GIANT
WHITETAILS
A LIFETIME OF LESSONS

MARK & TERRY DRURY

EDITED BY
MICHAEL HANBACK

Published by

kp **krause publications**

An Imprint of F+W Publications

700 East State Street • Iola, WI 54990-0001
715-445-2214 • 888-457-2873
www.krausebooks.com

Please call for our free catalog. Our toll-free number to place an order or obtain a free catalog is 800-258-0929 or please use our regular business telephone 715-445-2214.

Library of Congress Control Number:
2003111295

ISBN-13: 978-0-87349-737-4
ISBN-10: 0-87349-737-6

Edited by Michael Hanback
Cover photo by Mike Searles

Printed in China

CONTENTS

ACKNOWLEDGMENTS

Life has an interesting and unique way of steering you in different directions. Often you arrive at a fork in the road and choose one path over another for no more reason than a gut feeling. The path we have long traveled has led us around many turns and over many hills. But the one common thread along the way are the wonderful people who have supported our beliefs and goals throughout this lengthy journey.

First and foremost, we will forever be indebted to two of the most wonderful wives on earth. Along with our beautiful children and grandchildren, they have listened to more one-way telephone conversations – strategizing over a single deer for hours on a cell phone – than anyone should ever have to. They have seen camouflaged laundry strewn all over the place just waiting for it to dry. They've watched us methodically pack it all up into a huge bag only to drive off into the sunset leaving them standing in the doorway wondering how many weeks it will be before they see us again. Morning and evening, they've watched us plunk arrow after arrow into countless number of dilapidated targets. For years, they've dealt with muddy boots, dirty hats, wet clothes, shotgun shells, gun cases, bow cases, gloves, arrows, knives, flashlights, ropes, grunt calls, rattling antlers, mouth yelpers, box calls, deer heads, turkey mounts, photos, aerial maps, cameras, batteries, tripods and on and on. Their quiet, understanding thoughts are and forever will be held close to our hearts, for without the endless support and approval from our wives and children, the path we have chosen would be meaningless. We love them dearly.

It goes without saying that it all starts at the top. Our understanding parents and siblings have tolerated hunting conversations at every birthday party, wedding and holiday over the last 25 to 30 years. And they never complain, at least not in front of us, anyway. They too are a huge part of what we do and the sacrifices they have endured do not go without recognition. We thank them from the bottom of our hearts.

Also, countless friends, gracious landowners and business associates too numerous to mention, have played an important role in allowing us to do what we love best. Our hats are off to them. A thank-you is just not enough.

Finally, a sincere debt of gratitude goes out to our good friend Michael Hanback for converting our thoughts and words on countless pages as well as unending ramblings into a voice recorder into a work of art. Few can tolerate our overbearing hands-on approach in a business relationship, but he has done just that. He has miraculously deciphered unfinished sentences and dangling participles only to turn them into concise accurate accounts of actual occurrences so that others may benefit from our shortcomings.

Appropriately borrowing a line from our videos, we hope you enjoy this "production." It was created for you!

– Mark and Terry

INTRODUCTION

Like most people, we started hunting at an early age, around 9 or 10, cutting our teeth on rabbits and squirrels and eventually working up to wild turkeys and whitetails. Although we hunted with zest and became consumed with the great outdoors and nature's myriad wonders, we never realized we could actually make a living in the hunting industry.

In the mid-1980s, when the first mainstream outdoor videos hit the shelves, talented producers like Denny Gulvas and the legendary Wensel brothers of Montana inspired us. We ran out,

bought a camera and hit the woods. We'll never forget our first video encounter with a buck. Terry grunted it in, and whispered to Mark not to move and fool around with that darn camera. Terry proceeded to kill the buck, but not on film, while Mark sat watching the show! Our blood lust for hunting in the early days was hard to shake.

We evolved as both hunters and video producers, and we started Drury Outdoors in 1989. Since then, we have produced more than 100 big-game hunting films. About 75 percent of our video production business revolves around whitetails, and that percentage increases every year. The insatiable appetite of the American sportsman for deer hunting information never ceases to amaze us.

Recently, we've had a desire and a passion to branch out into books, because we wanted to share the unique tactics we've learned while hunting and observing whitetails for the past 30 years. We also wanted to focus on the deer hunting and management methods that have been so successful for us during the past decade. Publishing books made even more sense after we heard from many of our video fans who asked us for detailed information that only books can provide.

We are not writers, so we teamed up with our good friend Michael Hanback and cranked out our first book. We are proud of the fact that all the hunting tales and tactics found on these pages are based on our real-life experiences hunting 100 percent wild, 100 percent fair-chase whitetails. We're lucky to hunt deer from Sept. 1 to Jan. 31 each year in many habitats, mostly across our native Midwest. Along the way, we have learned the hard way from the best teachers in the world — thick-bodied, big-racked, fully mature bucks, the sight of which buckle your knees and send chills down your spine! When it comes to hunting big deer, we have made every possible error known to man. If this book can save one person from making the same foolish mistakes we've made, our efforts will be worthwhile.

As you read the book, keep in mind that we often ignore mainstream deer-hunting articles, videos, biologists and the like. Rather, we concentrate on the things we see and experience in the woods and fields, and then formulate our own opinions. Some of the information regarding the behavior, tendencies and movements of mature bucks cannot be found in books, magazines or videos. However, we strongly believe it because we have witnessed old, giant bucks doing these things time and time again.

Each chapter will begin by detailing the events of a giant whitetail we killed. Each chapter includes video clips reproduced as still photos from the actual hunt of these great bucks. We analyze everything about a whitetail, especially a mature buck, to the nth degree. Hunting these mature bucks is always a chess match. We don't know many other hunters who are quite as analytical and study the hunt like we do. Therefore, we are confident as each chapter concludes with our "Lessons Learned," you will find this information valid and helpful in your quest to harvest giant whitetails.

This book is certainly not the final work on deer hunting. Countless other individuals have differing opinions and techniques, and we have the utmost respect for all those folks. We have only conveyed what we truly believe. We don't want anyone to take this book for more than it really is — an accurate and enjoyable account of some of our most memorable, recent encounters with old, muscle-bound, heavy-racked bucks. However, we urge you to apply our tactics to your hunting area and situations. Hopefully one incident, tip or phrase from these pages will help you kill your next monster whitetail.

Read and enjoy. Just like all our Drury Outdoors videos, we produced this book just for you.

— *Mark and Terry Drury*
Summer 2003

CHAPTER ONE

A COLD OCTOBER WIND

You spend the hot, endless summer preparing. You shoot your bow repeatedly in the backyard, sweating profusely, plunking arrows into 3-D targets, tweaking sight pins, arrow shafts and broadheads – becoming robotic.

You make the long drive to your farms where you glass crop fields and grassy funnels at dusk and dawn, spotting as many whitetails as possible, shivering as you study the velvet racks of shooter bucks. You spend many hours pouring over aerial photos, pinpointing the bed-to-feed patterns of your quarry.

It goes on like that throughout the dog days of August and September, but you hang tough in brutal heat, knowing there's an end to the means. Soon it will be October and bow season. You have immediate visions of harvesting a giant whitetail.

Each year, Terry and I continue to learn the tricks of hunting the difficult month of October. Above all, we've consistently observed the first cold front of the month can be a magical time to be 20 feet up a tree. Let's begin with the story of a magnificent 6 1/2-year-old 12-point I shot one clear, windy afternoon. We know we're not the only ones who love those rare but wonderful October cold fronts. You know what we're talking about.

If only it were that easy.

The reclusive nature and nocturnal tendencies of mature bucks are as prevalent in early to mid-October as they are in any other month, maybe more so. It takes extremely favorable conditions to persuade a big deer to get up and walk during daylight.

Cool weather is one of those conditions.

The Weather Channel is on 24/7 at our hunting camps. When Terry and I see the "Weekly Planner" indicates the first cold front of October is streaming down from the north, we get as giddy as kids on Christmas Eve. Then the front blows through, bringing a trace or even an inch of rain and dropping the temperature 20, 30, maybe even 40 degrees. Our demeanors change when we step outside and into the high pressure on the backside of the front. The cool wind on our faces and the crisp air in our lungs rekindles our predatory instincts. We marvel at the crimson and golden leaves and the stunning mosaic they paint on the countryside. We are bundles of nervous energy. Our anticipation soars sky high when we think of what the next three months might hold. Fall has finally arrived, and we are bowhunters again.

Don't you just love that feeling?

Cool weather changes the psyche of mature bucks. Wrapped in big, thick coats, they don't move much when it's 70 degrees. But – BAM! – a cold front hits, and suddenly their internal cooling systems work again. Big deer get up and walk, searching for does and nudging them around. Cool weather makes deer more comfortable, just like it puts a skip in your step.

A few years ago, on Oct. 16, Terry and I skipped fast toward one of our favorite haunts. The first cold front arrived, dumping an inch of rain and dropping the temperature 30 degrees overnight. We awoke to a stiff, steady northwest wind bending the treetops, but that was all right. We can handle the wind, knowing full well that the cool, high-pressure on the backside of a front will kick the once-lazy deer into immediate action.

There was no doubt where to hunt that morning. When the wind rocks in early October, we don't see many deer moving in and around open fields or atop ridges. So we climbed to our stands in a low, wind-sheltered hollow where we suspected a good buck might be bedding. We didn't see one, but we jumped a few does while hiking back to the truck. A few deer were up and moving, and that revved our motors even more.

Terry and I spent the next several hours debating where to hunt the first prime, cool evening of the season. We had an opportunity here, and we didn't want to mess up. We considered myriad factors — wind speed and direction, general access to hunting areas, access to specific stand locations, and food sources and their proximity to bedding cover. We leave no stone unturned in our strategy sessions. Finally, we settled on another of our favorite spots – a stand set in a deep hollow.

We traveled the winding, narrow gravel drive up the hill and through the barnyard. Terry was careful not to rattle the old rusty chains that secured the gate. I cut the truck's engine, and we gathered our gear as quietly as possible. We clicked the doors shut ever so lightly.

October deer are different from November deer, and even December deer. Early season whitetails are super sensitive and on red alert. Make too much noise, or get sloppy and let deer see or smell you, and you'll clear a field or a nearby patch of timber. If a few deer run, they will all run. You will ruin your hunt before it ever begins, and you can contaminate a spot for weeks.

We slipped along a field edge, moving slowly and glassing up ahead, sidestepping fresh cow manure. Several times we paused to grind our boots in dry cow pies, a fine au naturel cover scent. Terry and I look for every advantage when chasing mature bucks.

We slipped through some nasty briars that rimmed the field and crossed a rusty barbed-wire fence. The wind whipped and gusted to 30 mph. Still, you can't be too careful when hunting early fall bucks. We took great pains to push down the top strands without making loud squeaks that might alert deer to our presence.

Then we stepped into the timber. It was like walking into a

church or museum. When Terry and I enter an old buck's domain, we do so with the utmost respect. And then we go into stealth mode, sharpening our senses to the nth degree.

The northwest wind rattled the trees, shook the leaves and helped conceal our approach. Still, we advanced toward the deep hollow cautiously and quietly, using giant hogbacks as cover. Our eyes flashed side to side like lasers. We expected to see white flags bounding away at any time. Deer bed frequently in the hollow's low, dense ground cover. It's common for deer to hold tight to their beds on windy days. We sneaked on, descending steadily, jumping no deer and feeling good about that. The lower we went, the more the wind died, until it felt like it was not blowing at all.

The hollow is an intriguing place. It runs northwest-southeast, and the terrain is deep and steep on both sides. We only hunt there during a northwest wind, because most of the deer come from the north and west, heading out of the bedding cover and moving toward fields of corn and soybeans 300 to 400 yards away.

We also only hunt there when the wind blows 20 to 30 mph up the hogbacks, and keeps on zinging through dark. That keeps air currents down in the hollow consistent. But on afternoons when the wind blows only 10 to 15 mph up top, the air swirls and gets squirrelly down where we hunt, so we stay out of there. Most people consider wind direction but fail to account for wind speed. However, it's just as important to know how much wind velocity a spot can handle.

As we neared the slope's toe, where the deep ravine adjoins the flat bottom, the terrain opened wide, like a gaping mouth. We immediately spotted the enormous fallen tree with a root wad nearly 10 feet in diameter. We crept straight to our landmark and veered toward our stands, taking as few steps as possible to cut down on noise and scent dispersal. We were especially careful to skirt downwind of trails where deer might walk in a couple of hours.

Down in the hollow, the stand setup is high off the ground. In fact, it's a real skyscraper, not for the weak of heart. Terry climbed first, shimmying up the tree like a squirrel. I noticed how careful he was not to drag his boots along the bark, not to make that awful, grating sound that might alert a bedded buck. You need to pay attention to such details, especially when hunting the super-sensitive deer of October. My brother high-stepped up, up and up, moving his body quietly and lightly with mere arm strength.

I shimmied up next and paused on the uppermost steps to examine the stand's straps and buckles. Everything was in order, so I stepped onto the platform, secured my safety harness and scanned the area for uninvited guests. Depending on how early a stand was hung in summer or early fall, it can make a nice refuge for ants, spiders, ground squirrels, yellow jackets and other pests that often claim squatter's rights to your property.

The first sit in an October stand is always interesting. Terry and I have climbed to our stands many times only to come face to face with some scary critters. Little camo parachutes would have been nice at those moments! But that day only a few mice called the foam seat home. I shooed them away and sat down.

Pulling up our gear takes time. It feels like an eternity! We just know a big buck is going to come along any minute and bust us before we get settled in. But we are diligent in our preparation. The ritual is a given, repetitive every time we climb into a set.

Terry checked and rechecked his camera's settings and filming angles as I pulled up my bow. I nocked my No. 1 arrow and checked its fletching and broadhead. I stood up, drew and swung slowly from side to side, checking every possible shooting lane. I let off, hung up my bow and snapped a couple of nearby limbs. I raised my binoculars and glassed the shooting holes for small, obscure twigs. It doesn't take much to deflect an arrow. Close inspection is always best.

I re-hung my bow, pulled out my laser range-finder and clicked away, checking every shooting lane, imprinting those yardages in my mind. After about 15 minutes, we were well-oiled machines, ready to hunt.

It wasn't long before the first deer appeared, sauntering down a trail, looking very relaxed.

"Year-and-a-half, coming straight to us," I whispered to Terry. He eased his camera toward the trail and hissed back, "All right, they're gonna move."

"Wait, I see another deer behind him," I whispered from beneath my binoculars. "Big deer, good buck. Oh man, a shooter!"

The buck meandered slowly along the trail, moving in super slow motion as mature deer often do in October. He repeatedly weaved left and right, but his overall course was south and east. I shivered, and my heart skipped a beat. From past observations in this stand, I knew that if the buck kept coming, he would meander down the hollow and end up directly below us.

The deer stopped, stared at a tree the size of your bicep and attacked it. For six or seven minutes, he rubbed, ripping the tree from top to bottom, lathering it with secretions from his eyes and forehead. He even licked it several times. It was one of the most incredible things we had ever seen!

As the buck worked, I calmed my nerves the best I could and glassed him. He was wide-eyed, but his full neck and especially the loose skin on his throat told us he was mature, very old. He had a unique look, with light-colored facial hair and a distinctive orange cap. And man, that rack! It was wide and heavy, glinting in the afternoon sunlight. Tall G-1s corkscrewed up, and the G-2s on either side were split. What character!

All at once, the buck stopped rubbing and looked up at his little buddy. The 1½-year-old buck had just tiptoed past us, and the big boy broke to follow him.

I nearly panicked. "Where am I going to get the shot?" I wondered, scanning the open holes along the trail, "Where can I kill this deer?"

He lollygagged all the way in, standard procedure for October movement, slow and methodical. Several long and excruciating minutes seemed like hours. Finally he was right there, 20 yards away. All those hours toiling, sweating and shooting in the backyard came in handy now. My Hoyt bow was an extension of my body as I drew and let fly.

The arrow hit with a sharp crack, squarely behind the buck's shoulder. But I was shooting a carbon shaft with an expandable broadhead, and it didn't pass through the deer. We watched him bolt hard and fast, with half the arrow sticking out. I slumped back on the seat, mentally drained.

Terry and I collected our thoughts and had a little celebration. We felt good about the hit, but we didn't see or hear the buck crash. His running hoofsteps just dribbled off to nothing. So we did what we almost always do in that situation, and you'll read about it over and over in this book — we left the buck alone. The steely light of dusk seeped into the hollow, and the temperature was dropping steadily. It was supposed to dip into the low 30s that night, so we felt doubly good about our decision.

We lowered our gear and shimmied out of the tree as silently as two guys can. The buck had actually run back toward our truck, so we made a big circle and went way out of our way so as not to jump him.

At one point on the hike, we heard rustling in the leaves. We immediately froze. Was it our buck? There was no way to know for sure.

Back at camp, Terry hooked up his video camera to a TV and we watched the hunt repeatedly. We felt even better about the hit now, but still that agonizing uncertainty swirled in our minds. It was another one of those long, sleepless nights.

The wind died overnight. The hollow was calm and chilly as a

mausoleum when we sneaked back in there at dawn. Within 100 yards of where we had heard the rustling the previous night, we found two blood-soaked beds. Then we found the buck.

He was a beautiful, ancient creature, and the kind Terry and I live to hunt. I knelt and held his great rack in my hands, tracing my fingers along his corkscrew brows and those split G-2s that gave him so much character. The light-tan hair and the orange cap on the buck's face and head glowed in the early morning sunshine.

That deep hollow is an awesome spot to hunt low when it's windy, but when a buck runs offs and dies down in there, you've got your hands full. Terry and I worked our butts off, wrestling the deer up and over rocks and logs, mostly dragging straight uphill. But it was a labor of love for my brother and me, and in an odd way we enjoyed every minute of it.

Thinking back over the history of Drury Outdoors, that was one of only two or three fully mature bucks we've killed in early to mid-October. That made the old, orange-capped, "corkscrew buck" even more special to both of us.

LESSONS LEARNED

Key on Cold Fronts. Each year, Terry and I extend our seasons by hunting in September in Western states like Montana, Wyoming and Kansas. Temperatures in those states can still be 80 to 90 degrees in early autumn. After hunting in the heat and anxiously awaiting Oct. 1 and the opening of bow season, we can't wait for that first fast-approaching cold front. We know it will make us – and the bucks – feel better.

We watch for that front on the Weather Channel, which stays on 24/7 in our camps. Once we see a front moving in from the north or northwest, we log onto weather.com. When you get used to surfing that site, you can look at the long-term weather forecast and then click on the detailed hourly forecast. The latter gives you great information, such as wind speed and direction on an hour-by-hour

We keep a keen eye to the sky awaiting that first magical October cold front.

basis. We use that all the time. We're fanatical about all facets of the wind. We need to know when and if the wind is going to switch so we don't get messed up when we're sitting in a stand. And we always want to know what the wind speeds are going to be from one day to the next. Such information allows us to plan on hunting high or low, like we did that afternoon when I killed the corkscrew buck.

ABOVE: Temperatures can drop from daytime highs in the 80s or 90s down to the 40s or 50s. Extreme drops really get deer on the move..

RIGHT: Calling can be especially effective during October's first front. We keep it light however if it's early in the month.

If the forecast tells us the wind is going to change — say at 8:30 or 9 a.m. — it has a bearing on where we elect to hunt that morning, and where we might move later on. You obviously don't want to keep hunting a stand when the wind changes, or you'll mess up a spot. If you know the wind is going to shift at a certain time, you can hunt one spot for a couple of hours and then move to another close, easily accessible stand when the wind turns.

Weather.com provides wind directions and speeds for 24- and 36-hour periods. You can use that information to plan one or two days' worth of hunting. Keep checking the Web site. The wind directions and speeds get more accurate the closer you get to hunting time. The data we get off the Web site is not 100 percent accurate, but we have had great results

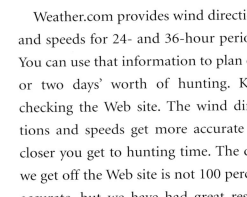

A benefit to hunting October often overlooked is the thick foliage allowing for a hidden approach to the stand.

with it thus far. It's become a crucial part of our hunting plan.

Furthermore, we always look for a barometer that's moving up or down. It usually falls before a front and rises after the front passes.

Deer often move steadily the day before a cold front. However, in October, we love to hunt just after a front blows through. We like temperature drops of 20 to 40 degrees with a front. The cooler it gets, the more deer we'll see. We think they feel an urgency to feed. In early to mid-October, deer move not to rut, but to feed. Cold temperatures make them walk before nightfall.

October thermals. We probably pay more attention to thermals in October than we do any other month. In fact, we plan our hunts more around where the thermals will push our scent than where the wind will drive it.

Consider a warm, calm October evening. When the sun goes down and the air cools and sinks, thermals push your scent down and away from your tree stand — and often smack into the powerful noses of those super-sensitive whitetails.

We've found that thermals are consistent in flat, open terrain. But when you hunt hilly or rolling terrain with some severe topographical changes, the thermals are near-

A 5 by side picked up in March can be the fuel needed to keep us going in October.

ly unpredictable. We've found out the hard way that thermals are hard to predict at the bases of ridges and in the mouths of valleys. The best you can do is hunt high in the morning, when the warm air and thermals rise, and low of an evening, when air cools and thermals push your scent down.

One last point: You can often predict if and when you'll have to deal with thermals at last light. Thermals typically are at work if the wind dies late in the afternoon and dips below 10 mph. However, if the breeze stays steady at 15 to 20 mph, thermals probably won't be as crucial.

LEFT: Packed up and heading out, so much of our hunting is done on the road. Our patented saying: "How much stuff does it take to kill a deer?"

Mother Nature
treats us to many
breathtaking
views throughout
October.

October Deer are Different. Over the years, we've noticed that October whitetails are super sensitive, even skittish. Their senses, especially smell, seem to be much keener than at other times of the year. That makes for tough hunting. You have to be extremely careful and cautious, and you have to pay close attention to details when choosing and accessing stands.

Deer also move slowly in October. Our hunt for the corkscrew buck is a great example. It took the old deer a long time to meander up the hollow and into shooting range.

We believe deer move slowly because they've been dealing with warm weather for months. The heat, along with their extreme sensitivity, puts deer in a slow-movement mode. It might take a buck an hour or 90 minutes to move 50 to 70 yards. He'll often stop to scent-check every twig, branch, rock and leaf. We see that a lot.

There will be many days when you'll have to sneak past four or five skittish does on the way to a stand, or let them slip past your perch before an old buck on red-alert shows up. It's a tough task that sometimes seems impossible.

Whitetails are natural browsers, and in October there's browse everywhere. That's another reason they move so

LEFT: The first cold air can affect your body more than any other all fall.

BELOW: Oh, how many times we climb a tree each fall. It gets tiresome by January, but in October we scurry up like squirrels.

slowly. It's also why they meander, veering here and there to eat and scent-check brush. If you arrived an hour earlier and rubbed up against that brush, there's a good chance deer will smell you and bust you.

Another thing we've noticed over the years is that deer do not bed very far from feed fields in October. Because summer foliage is still thick, a jungle in places, deer generally don't have to range very far to find security. That cover might be only 50, 100 or 150 yards off a food source. Generally, deer have bedded there, tight to the feed, all summer long. So if you penetrate 300 to 400 yards into an area, chances are you're going to walk right past — and probably spook — a buck you want to hunt.

Because a mature buck does-n't move far in October, you often need to set up close to where he beds, like Terry and I did on the hunt for the corkscrew buck. It's risky busi-ness, and when you try it, you must pay close attention to details.

First, make sure you've show-ered and are as clean and scent-free as possible. Maybe wear cover scent. Grind your boots in

dry manure or rinse them off if you cross a creek. Make no noise at the truck as you gather your gear. Don't rattle any chains. Don't squeak a fence. When a deer hits a barbed-wire fence, it twangs; when a person crosses it, it squeaks.

Use thick cover when accessing a stand. Hide behind hogbacks when sneaking in. Don't overlook ditches, creeks, etc. for disguising your approach.

When going to a stand, Terry and I always skirt it on the downwind side. Always! It's ultra-critical when hunting the sensitive deer of October. We never step on a trail, and we try not to cross one, even if it runs downwind of our stand. We want a buck to walk close and go broadside or step a few yards downwind for a quartering-away shot. Stay off those trails so deer won't smell you.

When we arrive at a tree, we don't loiter. We climb up and hoist up our gear as quickly and as quietly as possible. We try not to rake our boots on the bark. We make sure the seats on our stands never squeak. Nine times out of 10 in October, deer are bedded within earshot of where we hunt, so we take great pains to be as stealthy as possible.

TOP LEFT:
A happy hunter poses with an October trophy. The changing foliage always provides the perfect backdrop for photography.

BOTTOM LEFT:
Getting out and hunting ahead of November's hunting pressure allows for chasing good critters unaffected by man's presence.

On calm October afternoons, silence can be deafening. Those are the evenings when bucks move ever so slowly and cautiously. You have to move in and hunt with the mindset that deer are right there. You can't let your guard down, ever. You've got to stay in stealth mode. If you don't imagine that a good buck is just over the next hogback or down in the next hollow, you're probably going to

A single shed was one of the few clues that the reclusive buck even existed. The shed was found over $1/2$ mile from where we took the buck some 5 years later.

POSTSCRIPT

There's an interesting story behind the story of the corkscrew buck. Every time Terry and I watched the film of the hunt, the deer looked more familiar. We went back and reviewed some old footage we had shot years earlier. Those G-1s weren't as tall, but you couldn't miss their corkscrew configuration! When the deer was $3^1/2$ years old, Terry, much to his chagrin, had missed him with his bow. The heart-breaking miss had occurred within a 400-yard stretch of the hollow.

After that, the buck went underground. We found his sheds several times, but we didn't see him for three years, and we hunt that farm all the time. Then one afternoon, when the buck was $6^1/2$ years old, out he walks, rips apart a rub before our very eyes, and I'm lucky enough to get him.

It just goes to show how safe and secure a white-tailed buck gets after living for years in a particular area, like that deep hollow. Terry and I don't penetrate the hollow often — just when we get that first cold October wind.

make a mistake and spook him out of there.

One last note: Be smart when hunting 20 feet up a tree. If deer are bedded within 75 to 100 yards of your stand, you can get away with some slow, fluid movements. However, if you fidget around too much and make too many fast, herky-jerky moves, deer will pick you out every time. Terry and I have oftentimes climbed to our stands and spotted deer bedded nearby. It can be done. You just have to slip in quietly and cautiously. ■

Bring on that front!

CHAPTER TWO

I'VE GOT MY EYE ON YOU

For the Drury boys, most nights during hunting season turn into long and often boisterous strategy sessions. A few years ago – as Mark and I mapped out our options for the next morning's hunt – our nephew, Jared, rolled into camp. After bidding the usual hellos, the conversation immediately turned to, what else, giant whitetails!

I detected a gleam in Jared's eye as brother Mark and I rambled on about all the bucks we had seen on our Iowa farm. Jared perched himself on the edge of his chair and listened intently to our descriptive tales of mature deer with incredible body girths, bull-thick necks with loose-hanging skin and short, blocky faces with squinty eyes. Not missing a beat, we rolled into our bunks, babbling almost incoherently about tall tines, forked tines, sticker points, kicker points, drop tines and main beams as thick as axe handles.

■ To put us in the right place at the right time, Mark and I rely on countless hours of observing whitetails. This chapter unveils an incredible story of observation that resulted in a 20-yard bowshot at a 265-pound Iowa giant. We'll go in-depth on how you can become a better deer hunter simply by watching more and hunting less. Our observation tactics could be considered extreme. Our results, however, speak for themselves.

"I know that 3½-year-old 8-point down by the bottoms will score 140," Mark blurted, "and the 4½-year-old 9-point will go into the high 160s!"

"Yeah, and what about that hog we've been seeing walking through the gap and over into the CRP field?" I bellowed. "Man, that 10-point's pushing Boone and Crockett!"

"Whoa! Where are you guys seeing all these monsters?" Jared roared. He was totally into it by now, the gleam in his eye having turned to a blaze. "The 3-acre plot, the 6-acre? Is the swing-set field hot? How about the Biologic? "

Then it happened, like it always does during one of our big-buck powwows. We each darted to a dark corner of the house and dragged out heavy, overflowing boxes. Mark, Jared and I dug into the sheds like 6-year-olds tearing into presents at a birthday party. We strew the cast antlers all over the living-room floor, until it looked like a boneyard.

Tiny antlers, medium ones, gargantuan ones, we keep them all. Sheds are our souvenirs, and they tell us a lot about the home ranges and core areas of bucks that live on our farms. Sometimes we get lucky and find a deer's sheds two, three, maybe even four consecutive years. By finding sheds each March and then observing deer each summer and fall, we develop a strong and almost mystical connection with individual bucks. We literally watch them grow up. We've seen bucks grow 20 to 30 inches of bone on their heads in a single year. Amazing!

Jared hoisted up a heavy 4-point shed and asked, "Have you seen this bad boy yet this year?"

Mark stuck two giant, matching sheds to his head and laughed, "What in the world do you think this baby will look like this fall?"

It went on like that into the wee hours well after midnight, like it so often does.

Staying up too late just happens to be one of the only chinks in our defensive armor. It has caused us to "miss the bell" on more occasions than we care to divulge, but that's another story. Suffice to say, we overslept and awoke late for the next morning's hunt. However, it didn't faze us. We've overslept before, and while we hate to do it, we've learned to accept it. Besides, the moon was rising around 2 p.m. during this October stretch, making hunting better in the evenings anyway. Later in this book you'll read more about how we love to hunt during a rising moon.

We might oversleep, but we never bag a morning hunt. We simply roll right into Plan B. After throwing on our Mossy Oak camouflage and cramming caps over our disheveled hair, we made some last-minute decisions. Having lost the cover of darkness, we had to choose stands with easy access, and where we could slip in undetected.

Jared went to "the strips" strictly to observe deer. He carried his Handycam so he could capture footage of any deer he spotted. Mark and I would try to sneak in and hunt the "6-acre" set on the

southerly wind. The Biologic was lush and green there, and deer were browsing on it before going to bed each day. Maybe we would get lucky and catch a buck staying up late, too.

I drove like a madman, burning up the gravel roads and leaving huge plumes of dust in my wake. Mark and I gathered our gear, went into stealth mode and crept toward the stand. We almost made it. We rounded a point and spotted the set. Trouble was, there were deer between it and us.

I glassed several does and small bucks lingering in the field and then turned my attention to a pretty good 8-point. I studied his lean muscular body and neck. He

reminded me, physique-wise, of a well-trained racehorse. We figured he was 3¹/₂ years old. His rack was particularly wide, about 20 inches, and we reckoned it would score 135, give or take a few inches.

We immediately shifted into Plan C. We sneaked to a makeshift ground blind, and as Mark readied his camera, I readied my rattling antlers. What the heck, it was worth a shot. It was late October, and the bucks were getting a little wide-eyed and starting to nose does around a bit.

I cracked the antlers, giving my best rendition of moderately aggressive sparring. The buck looked our way, dropped his head and went back to feeding. I could have sworn he yawned! I floated a few grunts, rattled some more, and then cut loose a nasally snort-wheeze. The deer ignored it all and meandered out of the field and into the timber.

We struck out, but with Mark filming over my shoulder and from ground zero, we captured a pretty cool encounter with the buck. We also learned something. We spotted a deep ditch just back in the timber that paralleled the field and pointed straight toward the stand. We could use that ditch for quick, easy access to the set on another morning, especially, heaven forbid, if we overslept again!

For each hunt, it's important to observe and analyze not only deer movement,

but also other things like terrain breaks that might come in handy the next day, the next week or the next season. As long as you're learning, a day in the timber is never a bust.

Although our hunt was uneventful, Jared had a morning to remember. He slipped into the strips undetected and climbed into one of our box blinds. It's an awesome late-season gun stand, but we also go there a lot during archery season just to glass, watch and study the movements of does and bucks. The blind is elevated and gives the observer a fantastic view of the corn, soybeans, timber edges and strips of brush.

Minutes after climbing the blind's awkward steps and taking great pains not to let the swollen plywood door squeak, Jared settled into a rusty, metal chair and prepared his Handycam for action. He didn't have to wait long. A basket-racked, $1^1/_2$-year-old old buck appeared in the cut corn and started feeding. Then, in a small strip of standing corn, Jared noticed some of the stalks were wiggling. Suddenly, out strides a hog-bodied 10-point! His rack was wide and heavy, with G-3s that shot up like daggers. The buck was a fighter. His left G-2 was snapped plum off near the base.

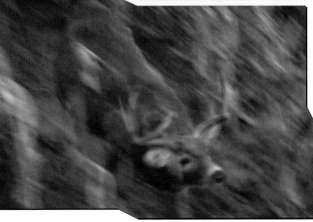

Jared calmed his racing heart and videoed the monster for about 20 minutes before he and his little buddy skulked off into the timber, finally going to bed. However, the deer had stayed up late enough so that our nephew could get some vital information. Just spotting the bruiser was one thing. Better yet, Jared had honed in on the exact spot where the big boy walked into the cut corn.

Jared was pumped when he met us back at camp later that morning. He burned some fantastic footage and couldn't wait for his uncles to see it. He hooked his camera to the monitor, cracked a smile and hollered, "What do you think of that hog?!"

As the muscle-bound buck strode across the TV screen, Mark screeched, "I know that deer! I observed him in velvet back in July. We've got some of his sheds around here somewhere. He's even bigger than I thought. Man, he'll go 150!"

Mark also noted that one of our close friends, Dave Reisner, filmed the same buck out of the same box blind a couple of weeks earlier. Dave's footage showed the buck in a distant bean field. The deer would have undoubtedly come closer and fed in the corn and beans had some coyotes not spooked him by appearing at the most inopportune time.

Let's see, three solid sightings of the buck in the same area, two of those recent and the last viewing was super-hot, having occurred only hours earlier. Jared could see the wheels spinning in our minds and he chirped, "If the wind stays right, and it's supposed to, I'd go back and hunt that buck if I were you guys. He felt awfully comfortable there, and I'd almost bet he will be back."

That was all the prodding we needed. We had a new setup about 200 yards from the box blind. Mark and I would be sitting in it later that afternoon.

We sneaked in there at 2 o'clock. I thought that by arriving early that afternoon it might somehow compensate for getting up late that morning. Oh well, it never hurts to be in your stand and ready for action.

We climbed up and then it struck me. This was the spot Mark had been so darn adamant about hunting all fall. Several times over

the past couple of months, he had told me, "Terry, we're going to kill a big buck out of that tree, I just know it." He kept repeating himself so much that it was almost comical.

When you hear big talk like that you think, "Yeah, it could happen." But you are always somewhat skeptical, never fully convinced that it will happen.

Brother Mark is a mad scientist when it comes to creating funnels and inside corners for deer. He selected this tree way back in May, and then planted his food plots accordingly. He planted corn out from the tree in one direction, and beans in another direction. Therefore, he created an inside corner where bucks could cut across

the field, turn and then walk either edge straight into bow range.

Maybe it could happen. I gazed up at the moon, big and fluorescent in the clear-blue sky. Deer just might move early and hard toward the food plots this evening.

It was a long sit, and we didn't see a deer until 45 minutes before dark. Then out popped a yearling buck. You couldn't miss that tall but miniature basket rack. It was the same little deer Jared taped this morning. The youngster cornered through the beans and then the corn and walked within 15 yards of our stand.

"I told you this was the spot," Mark whispered.

Excited, we shifted our predatory instincts into overdrive. The yearling's heavyweight buddy must be somewhere around, but where? We glassed like wild men.

There! The giant buck with the snapped-off tine popped out of a draw about 100 yards away, perfectly upwind. He strode across the field like he owned the joint, muscles rippling and hips swiveling. I clipped my release to the bowstring. Suddenly, he turned and disappeared into the standing corn to our left.

Our hearts sank faster than the Titanic. We sat in silence and were convinced it was not going to happen, at least not this night. You probably know that feeling all too well.

"Oh, Terry!" Mark hissed. "There he is, right there – right where Jared spotted him this morning!" I cut my saucer-wide eyes to the monster standing 30 yards away. He was in the edge of the cut corn, ogling a doe out in front of him. All at once, he tilted back his head, thrust his nose into the air and charged her.

The doe sprinted to the middle of the field like she was shot out of a cannon. The enormous buck took off after her and then, for some strange reason, stopped 20 yards from our stand. Maybe there was something special about this tree. I could chew on that later. There was still tedious, nerve-racking work to be done.

I drew my bow and locked onto the 20-yard pin. The aluminum arrow sizzled through the air and

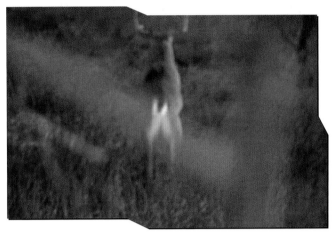

struck the buck with a mighty whack.

I hit him hard, maybe a little low and back, but still squarely in the boiler room, I was certain. The deer bolted low and fast across the field and topped a grassy hill, his spectacular rack riding high. He then vanished into the timber. We didn't see him fall, and again we did the right thing. The temperature was dropping, and the buck would keep. Why risk it? We climbed out of our set and headed home for another one of those long, sleepless nights.

The next morning was picture perfect for October: crisp and bright. As soon as we stepped into the color-splashed timber, I spotted the buck, his huge, white belly facing us, shining in the morning sun. I ran over there and put my hands on the monster. His body was even bigger than we had thought! He weighed, on the hoof, at least 265 pounds. Even missing one long G-2, his heavy, dark rack scored a solid 150. He was a magnificent deer and yet another testament to the awesome power of observation.

LESSONS
LEARNED

Observatory Tactics. Mark and I watch deer many more days than we actually hunt them each year. If you can break out of a strictly hunting mode and become more of an observer, you will become a better and more successful hunter.

We keep quality binoculars around our necks pretty much year-round. We observe deer when we're hunting sheds in March, calling turkeys in April and planting food plots in May. In spring, bucks obviously don't have big racks, but we hone in

It's a special bond that's formed in a tree between cameraman and hunter. How many hours do we spend 20 feet off the ground? We're afraid to tally it!

on their physiques, which is a better indicator of maturity. Spot an old deer and observe his movements anytime during the year, and it gives you vital information about his home range and core area.

We get down to business in late July and throughout August and September. I can't tell you how many hundreds of miles we put on our trucks running back and forth between our farms and how many hours we tally with binos crammed in our faces. I just know my eyes hurt as we observe deer in crop fields and Biologic plots. Many mature bucks become visible when coming to feed and showboat for other deer. We enjoy ogling their big racks, velvet in the summer and polished and gleaming later in September, but we go way beyond that. We look for the exact corners, edges or funnels where most mature bucks enter fields. We cross-reference those entry points against aerial photographs and formulate our hunting plans for fall. We are always looking to pinpoint weaknesses.

Many hunters glass fields during evenings, but they forget about mornings. Not Mark and I, unless we oversleep! You need to observe deer in funnels, along edges and cutting back across weed-choked fields as they move from the feed fields to their bedding areas. You simply can't watch bucks too much as you try to pattern them.

Most days we watch deer through binoculars and spotting scopes. Buy the best optics you can afford. You need quality,

Sometimes we observe with cameras, other times it's with binoculars or spotting scopes.

light-gathering glass to pick up the really big boys that typically move in the twilight of dawn and dusk.

We have the luxury of filming many of the bucks we observe. Then we go home and roll the footage, studying the maturity of the bucks' bodies and scoring their racks. You can do it, too. Carry your home video camera and capture some footage of the bucks you observe. Then watch the deer. Study their patterns. It will not only get you pumped for bow season, it will also help you become much better at field-judging the ages and racks of deer.

Personal observation is impossible in many of our thick, secluded honey holes, so we do the next best thing. In out-of-the-way spots, we set up Trail Mac cameras and photograph mature bucks skulking in and out of the areas. We'll go in-depth on using trail cameras in Chapter 10.

Mark and I are so fortunate to have some great friends and pro-staffers for Drury Outdoors. These guys and gals graciously give up a lot of their spare time and vacation days to help us observe deer. You can't be everywhere at once. You and your buddies can do the same. Split up and observe all the corners of your hunting area. When you get together and compare notes, it gives you the big picture of how many mature bucks are roaming the property and how and where they are moving between food sources and bedding areas. Then you can put your heads together and set into motion a hunting plan that benefits everyone.

If deer are visible from a gravel road, Mark and I pull over and glass 'em. When that's not an option, we hide our trucks and, using cover or structure, creep to a good vantage point that overlooks a mosaic of edges, food plots, creek bottoms, grassy

funnels and other travel routes. That vantage might be up on a hill or ridge. A string of big, round hay bales can be a good observation post for sprawling feed fields. The last thing we want to do is pressure a gnarly old buck, so wherever we set up, we try to stay at least 400 yards away.

In the right situation, if we can slip in silently and without deer seeing us, we observe from one of the gun-hunting blinds we have scattered across our farms. We often hang tree stands with a long-range view of quality deer habitat. We particularly like the latter tactic, which allows us to stay mobile and

Nothing gets overlooked. We study aerials for hunting sights, access routes and wind directions. The key to effective observation is never allowing them to know they're being observed.

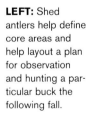

LEFT: Shed antlers help define core areas and help layout a plan for observation and hunting a particular buck the following fall.

RIGHT: Often times we watch from our vehicles if the deer are visible from a county road. We also watch for other hunters who might try to sneak in on a buck.

check several areas.

Many people think their work is done after they spot a big deer once or twice. They figure they know where to hunt him. Not Mark and I. We rely heavily on multiple observations. We try to spot a mature buck as many times as possible – sometimes with the help of our friends – watching, analyzing and pinpointing the deer's movements. We are forever looking for that exact, sweet spot to bowhunt him.

A lot of what we have talked about here deals with summer observation. However, we also use our deer-spotting tactics into October, November and beyond. Before we hang a bowhunting stand, hours of preparation must point us to a particular tree. And then we're still not done. The conditions must be perfect before we move in and hunt that stand — the weather, the rising or falling moon, and especially the wind speed and direction.

I've got my eye on you!

Shed-Hunting. Mark and I have become nearly as fanatical about shed-hunting as we are about observing deer. We've learned that when you put the two awesome tactics together, you

Good observation can put you in the right spot when winds turn favorable.

Early morning observation helps determine travel routes from food to bed.

can really pinpoint core areas and specific movements of mature bucks.

We start looking for sheds as soon as the snow melts. In the Midwest, most bucks cast their antlers between the first week of February and the second week of March. We glass fields in late January to see where most bucks are hanging out, and to learn how many of them have dropped their antlers. We search for sheds as soon as possible, because ground squirrels and other critters can chew off tines in a hurry. We also look for sheds when we hunt turkeys in April and plant crops and Biologic plots in May.

Hunt hard for sheds around food plots and

Some hidden spots don't allow for personal observation. Our Trail Mac cameras serve as fantastic substitutes.

A mature non-typical 180" 14 pt. buck working a scrape. This picture was taken on December 14th.

Before we hang a stand much preparation must point us to that tree. Aerial photography, wind direction and diligent observation are all taken into consideration.

Our observation tactics are sometimes extreme. Our results speak for themselves.

crop fields where deer concentrate in winter. If you have access to standing corn or soybeans, those are dream spots to find sheds.

If you're still out there glassing in late January or early February, pay close attention to where bucks enter and leave fields. Bucks often walk 100 yards or so and lie down on east or south slopes. You can often find sheds there. As a side note, we only enter prime bedding areas, or what we call "sacred grounds," when shed-hunting in spring. You should do the same. When entering a prime bedding area, look around, analyze the cover configuration and look for the easiest ways a big buck can enter and exit the area. That information will come in handy when you return in fall.

Most people are pumped if they find one or two big sheds each spring, and they should be. Well, brother Mark and I are disappointed if, after walking our tails off, we don't find 30 or 40! To hit the mother lode of sheds, you need to look real close. We often use a grid search. Mark off a 20-yard grid and cover every inch of it before moving on to the next grid.

Rainy days are great for shed-hunting. It's unbelievable how antlers shine when it's wet. Harsh sunlight is the worst — it makes sheds tough to spot.

Evening observation helps us determine exactly where deer move onto feed fields. Good glass is a must for low light when the oldest bucks move.

LEFT: A distant hay bale serves as the perfect vantage point. More often than not we observe at a distance of 400 yards or more.

Most people look right over sheds. They look way too far out in front of where they're walking. Take it real slow and look straight down at the ground, scan every square foot. Sometimes you'll spot a whole antler, or maybe just a tine. Some sheds are white, while others are brown and blend with grass and leaves. You've got to look close. We've often stepped on a shed or walked right past them. Take the time to turn around and scan the area you have just walked through. A different perspective with different lighting can yield huge results.

We keep every shed we find, from spikes to big 4- and 5-point sides. We also record when and where we find them. We occasionally pull out the souvenirs, scatter them on the floor and evaluate them. That's how we oftentimes learn big-buck patterns.

We've found a buck's sheds two, three, even four years in a

row. And we've found some of them in the same 50- to 100-acre patch of timber. That tells us a lot about a buck's home range and core area. And it certainly tells us where we should focus our energies during hunting season.

The following is a true story, I swear. I shot that giant Iowa buck, the stunning centerpiece of this chapter, on Oct. 26. Well, I killed him 50 yards from where our friend Don Kisky picked up the buck's sheds earlier that spring. Incredibly, the buck had grown 30 inches of antler from age $2\frac{1}{2}$ to $3\frac{1}{2}$. ∎

This matched set of sheds was picked up by Don Kisky within 50 yards of where Terry shot the buck on October 26th later that year. The buck had grown 30" from age $2\frac{1}{2}$ to $3\frac{1}{2}$.

POSTSCRIPT

It was a happy ending for more than just the obvious reasons. However, there's another fantastic story within the story of the muscle-bound buck.

That afternoon, Jared went back to the box blind where he had spotted the huge deer that morning. The southeast wind was perfect for the set, so he wouldn't have interfered with our plans. To the contrary, Jared tried to help us even more. His plan was to film the evening hunt from a distance, with the remote possibility of catching the action on tape from an

RIGHT: Jared captures the action from his perch that evening. A southeast wind allowed for a double camera set up.

BELOW: Our nephew Jared sat in a late season gun stand to film the huge 10-point from 200 yards.

entirely different angle. "Double filming" was something we had never tried before in the history of Drury Outdoors, at least not with a giant whitetail.

Well, Jared made history. While Mark was filming at the scene, Jared was rolling tape from off to the right. On Jared's footage, the viewer can see my arrow coming out of the trees to the left and then vanishing into the deer. It went in white, came out red and kicked up dirt and corn stalks on the other side of the mega buck. Tremendous! To this day, it's the only bow-kill we've ever captured with two cameras.

Through a combination of observation and stunning cinematography, Jared and Mark did all the work that incredible October day. I was simply the lucky recipient of all their efforts. There's nothing like being spoon-fed every once in a while.

Thanks guys!

CHAPTER THREE

ONE WAY OUT

S ex, drugs and rock 'n' roll have absolutely nothing to do with deer hunting. Or do they?

In the 1970s and '80s, hard rock took America by storm, and Foghat was one immensely popular band. As the song "Slow Ride" soared to the top of the charts, we could have never imagined that

one day we would share a hunting lease with an original member of that legendary band. It's funny how the love of deer hunting can bring unusual acquaintances together.

Out of respect for his personal identity we'll refer to this fine gentleman as Hot Rod. Because Rod is unselfish and always willing to help others, he once drove Terry out to show him one of the best spots on the new lease. As Rod's truck bounced in and out of potholes along the old dirt road, Terry won-

> Whitetails use complex networks of trails and funnels to move to and from bedding areas and food sources. In many situations, structure or dense cover converge and make deer patterns more predictable. These situations often bring does and bucks within bow range. This chapter, which showcases the largest buck of our lives, details how to find, use and even create ultimate deer funnels. Terry and I hold nothing back as we share one of our most effective tactics.

dered, "Where in the world is he taking me?" Most of the property was huge agricultural fields along the Mississippi River. It didn't seem to have much timber.

Hot Rod rolled his truck to a stop alongside a levee that snaked for miles. This manmade levee was constructed to protect the fertile crop fields from floods. After climbing to the top of the levee, Hot Rod confidently smiled and asked, "So what do you think; care to walk it?"

Terry didn't hesitate. "I think it's awesome," he replied, gazing across the vast river bottom. He could now see two timber blocks, one about 150 acres and the other about 20 acres. Both blocks appeared to be whitetail havens. Most intriguing was a massive brush pile that workers had bulldozed up against the larger wood-lot when making room for the earthen levee. The structure was about 15 feet high and ran the entire length of the timber.

Hot Rod and Terry hiked into the giant hardwoods and did some speed scouting. They found several giant rubs and a maze of trails that zigzagged through the bottom. Deer seemed to meander with no set patterns, as they seldom do in a flat, open river bottom. It would be difficult to select a stand site.

Hot Rod led Terry through the timber and stopped at the first big opening in the brush pile. My brother really honed in on that spot. The timber was on one side of the brush wall, and the feed fields and the levee were on the other side. A light bulb flashed in Terry's head. "There's only one way out!" he exclaimed. The bottleneck was littered with fresh tracks and droppings. The logical choice for a stand location was simple, but would a mature buck walk through the opening during daylight or stage up until the intense pressure of does, fawns and young bucks had passed?

To stay consistent with our low-impact approach, Hot Rod and Terry hustled out of the timber and drove away. Terry thanked Rod for his help, and they bid their farewells. On the way home, all Terry could think about was the long windrow and his one-way-out theory. Terry pondered the unique situation for hours then jumped into his truck and drove back to the river bottom. He headed straight to the opening with all the sign.

Terry analyzed the situation while backtracking the winding brush wall. He suspected mature bucks probably scent-checked the timber from the downwind side when they returned to their morning bedding areas and while traversing evening feeding routes. He also suspected bucks used the brush wall as security to enter and exit such areas.

The farther away from the opening Terry walked, the less intense the deer trails became, until they diminished completely. He then spotted a glowing rub line with big, thrashed trees 100 to 150 yards apart that ran just 20 yards parallel to the brush wall. There were only a few sets of tracks on the faint trail, but one set was enormous. They led into and out of a logged area that had grown over with low, thick cover.

Terry backed 150 yards off the bedding area and picked out a straight, beautiful maple as a stand site. The tree was a safe distance from the bedding areas, which allowed us undetected access. He hung our stands within minutes and then anxiously raced home and called me.

"Mark, I've found the spot," Terry hollered into the phone. "I can almost guarantee we'll kill a big deer there. You wouldn't believe all the big rubs. The set is awesome for a northwest wind, because deer can't get downwind. A monster buck is using this trail frequently; you won't believe the tracks I cut. They're huge!"

I had never heard my brother so pumped, and his enthusiasm was contagious.

This lease is in a part of Illinois where a southwest wind pre-dominates throughout October. We waited for a warm breeze to switch, but it didn't. We heard the rut might come early in Wisconsin, and as luck would have it, Terry had drawn an archery tag up there. We drove north from our homes in Missouri and Iowa and hunted several days. Unfortunately, extreme heat gripped the Badger State, too, and bucks weren't moving. That only revved our motors to return to Illinois and hunt the new lease with all those big rubs and gargantuan tracks. We drove all night and got back before dawn on Oct. 30.

We hurriedly dressed in our Mossy Oak camo and checked the

wind. It still wasn't right, so we hunted another farm. We didn't see a deer. Then, around lunchtime, a small front moved in. The sky grew overcast, the breeze turned out of the northwest, and Terry bellowed, "Pack up, brother, we're going to the spot!"

We were finally fixing to hunt the river bottom I had heard so much about. And to top it off, I was the shooter. Because I had filmed Terry in Wisconsin, I was now "in the can."

My first impression of the spot was, "Man it's awesome!" The river bottom was pristine. You could look down through the silvery trees and imagine a buck coming, his heavy rack glinting in the afternoon sunlight. I had renewed hope with visions of grandeur!

"Check that thing out," Terry whispered, pointing to the long, towering brush pile that bordered the levee. It was one of the most unusual deer funnels I had ever seen. Then he pointed to the faint trail laced with rubs and huge tracks. He also explained how there were several small gaps in the brush where bucks could cut through the windrow and enter the cropfield at a considerable distance from our location.

"I know several bucks are using this trail," Terry whispered, reading my mind, "and it would have been easy to hang stands by the gaps where the sign is heavy. But I kept cutting this giant track, and I followed it along the windrow to the east end of the bottom. Up there the adjacent landowner has done some clear-cutting, and it's a jungle. The trail's faint, but that big track keeps cutting in and out of the cover. We are set up within earshot of the bedding area just a few yards of the trail leading to it."

Terry had done the legwork and then some. He'd sawed a path up and over a giant pile of logs and brush, so we made little noise as we sneaked in and climbed to our stands. I readied my gear and looked around — open bottomland on one side, tight cover to my right. The best part was, with a northwest breeze, deer could not get downwind of us because of those brush piles.

My stand was fine, but Terry wondered, "I don't know about the filming angle, think I can move?"

"Go for it," I replied. You should never be afraid to tweak your setup when bowhunting a big deer. Your first time in is almost always the best. Terry pulled his stand from a nearby tree and hung it in the maple above mine, where he could film over my shoulder and communicate a little easier.

We talked and laughed in whispers throughout the afternoon, like we always do. We had fun, but didn't see a deer. At about 4:45 p.m., Terry said, "Why don't you rattle?"

I thought, "Late October, pre-rut, keep it short and sweet." So, I tickled the antlers briefly.

Twenty minutes later, with the evening light dimming, Terry whispered, "Rattle again. And this time let 'em know we're here." The action was slow, but I could tell from the tone in my brother's voice that he was still pumped about the spot.

I clicked the antlers and threw in some snort-wheezes. Then I figured, 'What the heck?' I rattled as hard as I could for a while, and then sat down.

Sitting down … That's something I never do! After calling, I always stand on the platform and hold my bow, just in case a buck approaches fast or is bedded nearby.

I don't know why I sat down that evening. But I do know it almost cost me the buck of a lifetime.

I gazed down the river bottom. Nothing. When I looked back to the right — there stood an enormous buck! Where had he come from? How had he slipped in without making a sound? I was

stunned and just sat there in near shock. Then I hugged the tree with my back, eased up the stand seat and stood up. Somehow the deer didn't see or hear me.

"Terry, there's a 180-inch buck standing at 20 yards on the trail," I whispered, my voice quivering as I reached for my bow.

"Yeah, right," he grinned.

We cut up and bust each other all the time, saying stuff like, "Huge buck, get your bow!" But this was the real deal, and Terry didn't believe me.

"I swear there's a 180 at 20 yards," I pleaded. Terry turned on his camera, but he still didn't buy it. For the next 90 seconds on the tape's audio you hear all this whispering, mostly me panicking and trying to convince my brother I wasn't kidding. I kept cutting my

eyes down to the buck. He was in the wide open, but a big maple tree blocked Terry's view.

I could hardly stand it. "Terry, I swear on Taylor's life there's a 180-inch buck 20 yards away!"

My brother stopped smiling and immediately changed his demeanor. When I swore on my daughter's life, he knew I was serious.

The buck stood, moving his head rapidly, looking left, right, left, right for the "deer" he heard fighting. It was the longest five minutes I can remember in hunting. It was tough to stare at the buck, especially his giant rack, for so long. But on the other hand, it gave me time to calm down and get over the shock of, "Oh my gosh, monster buck, got to

shoot!" I actually decelerated emotionally, thinking, "I'm not going to get a shot. This big deer's gonna turn and run away."

The buck moved closer and cleared the maple. Terry shivered, but his camera whirred. The deer came closer, looking mad and grunting every other step. He stopped 5 yards from our tree. He was straight down but quartering slightly on, so I didn't draw.

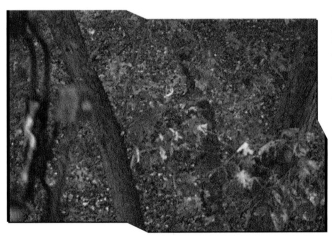

Suddenly, the buck snapped his head up and worked some branches with his rack and face. He looked straight up! I gasped, but somehow he didn't bust us.

The deer lowered his head and ripped a scrape.

I'd had about all I could stand. I'd studied every inch of the 10-pointer's rack, including five stickers. I thought, "God, he might be bigger than 180!"

The deer took two steps. I put tension on the bowstring. "Please keep coming," I pleaded, "I'll have a broadside shot at 10 yards."

I sensed a change in the buck's demeanor. He was tentative, probably because he'd left his security cover and couldn't get downwind

of my rattling. And he didn't see any deer fighting next to his bedroom. The buck dropped his head like he was going to step forward, but in a flash he turned and headed back into the thicket.

I drew and bleated with my voice. The buck stopped, but all I could see was butt and guts. I took a full step out on the edge of my stand, leaned and twisted some more. I could see the buck's last three ribs through a small hole in the cover.

I squeezed off the shot and watched the arrow hit. It looked good, halfway up and through the last ribs of the quartering-away buck. He mule-kicked and crashed away fast, another good sign. After we settled down, caught our breath and stopped shaking, Terry and I high-fived and hugged each other several times.

It was dark when our feet hit the ground. We found the blood-soaked arrow and retreated immediately. With a deer like that, you don't take any chances.

We hurried out of the woods and back to the cabin where we were staying. The place had an old TV and VCR, and we couldn't get the darn things to work.

"We've got to see this footage!" Terry roared. We loaded up the camera and headed for Wal-Mart.

Carrying our equipment into the store, we hooked it up to several TVs before finding one that worked. As we watched the footage, some guy walked up and said, "Man, what a buck! Way to go!" We bought the TV, took it back to the cabin and reviewed the hit over and over.

The shot looked good, and we were sure we had the buck. Still, we didn't want to push things. The weather front that had moved in at lunchtime had dropped the temperature significantly. It was plenty cold, so we decided to leave the buck overnight.

At first light the next morning, we cut a good blood trail and followed it for about 250 yards. We expected to stumble across something any minute, and we did. A coyote ran straight at us!

"Terry, they've found the buck," I yelled. "He's got to be right here somewhere."

Now frantic, we pressed on. No deer. The blood trail led out of the woods and into a cut cornfield. We looked at each other as our hearts sank. No way a mortally wounded buck should leave cover for open ground.

The mind games began. I doubted the shot, the hit, everything. Emotionally, it was the lowest of the lows.

We followed drops of blood into the field, where it finally pooled and stopped. We looked for two hours on hands and knees. Nothing.

"Let's go get some help," Terry finally whispered.

I agreed.

It was a tough time, and my brother tried to stay upbeat. "I'm still praying we'll find this deer," he said.

"Me too," I replied. "I'll do anything to find that buck. I'll give up all my bad habits, change my ways, whatever." And I meant it.

Terry looked across the bottom, pointed in the direction of the truck and led the way. We had just left the field and stepped back into the timber when he jerked around, grabbed my shoulders and shouted, "Look!"

There was blood everywhere – almost as if a deer had gone on a death run.

I looked up and saw the buck lying 30 yards away. Screaming, I ran to him. I held the huge antlers in my hands and cried. It had

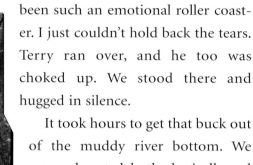

been such an emotional roller coaster. I just couldn't hold back the tears. Terry ran over, and he too was choked up. We stood there and hugged in silence.

It took hours to get that buck out of the muddy river bottom. We were exhausted, both physically and mentally, when we got back to the cabin. However, it was Halloween, and we were determined to get home to our families. I called my wife, Tracy, with the good news. We quickly loaded our truck and began the two-hour drive to our parents' house.

It amazes me how a big whitetail draws a crowd. The buck caused a traffic jam at the check station. People huddled around to see it. Our friend Stan Potts, an official scorer, met us there and put a tape to the buck. The rack was 20 inches wide, had 30-inch main beams, and had more than 21 inches of mass per side. The 10-pointer, with five abnormal points, grossed 195 $^1/_8$ and netted 184 $^2/_8$ nontypical inches.

Terry and I looked at each other and smiled. We keep close tabs on the hunting industry, and we knew this buck was the largest-grossing whitetail ever killed with a bow on video at the time.

We then stopped in St. Louis to show the buck to our friend Steve Stoltz. Three truckloads of guys had spotted the rack sticking out the truck bed, and they pulled off the highway to check out the deer and offer their congrat-ulations. It was a wild ride.

We arrived at Mom and Dad's at around 9 p.m. The trick-or-treat-ing was pretty much over, but the party had begun. Some 40 friends and family members, including my wife and daughter, Taylor, showed up to the see the buck. Terry rolled the video, and a big cheer went up at the shot.

From a business standpoint, shooting a buck like that on film is a huge accomplishment. But to have shared the hunt with my brother, and then to have celebrated the occasion with so many people so close to us, made it even more special. It's something I'll never forget.

There's one last thing. Somewhere along the way I measured the old buck's hoof. It taped 7+ inches from the tip of the hoof to the relaxed dewclaws. It had to be the monster whose tracks Terry and Hot Rod had found on the lease a month earlier.

BILL MARCHEL

LESSONS
LEARNED

Identify Deer Funnels. Funnels come in all shapes and sizes. Most are natural features of the topography. Others, such as that long windrow on the Illinois lease where we killed our biggest buck ever, are manmade. Your job is to identify and discover funnels that affect deer travel. Typically, the best funnels are littered with trails, tracks, rubs and scrapes. Hang a stand near a hot funnel, and when the wind is right, go in and hunt a mature buck on natural movement.

This pretty 8 pt. walked within 10 yards of a north wind set because of an eroded ditch.

Most terrain funnels we look for are located on or around ridges. One of our favorites is where two hog-backs, or finger ridges, come together and peter out in a drainage. A spot like that is a great dumping ground for deer, although it's difficult to get a consistent wind to hunt. We also look for low saddles or bottlenecks where a wide ridge narrows down considerably. Sometimes these slight nuances concentrate does and younger bucks. Be forewarned the older a buck gets the less likely he will walk through a constrained area. Mature bucks often approach these areas from down-

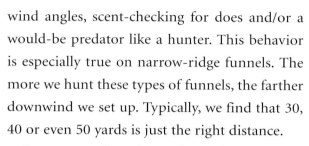

wind angles, scent-checking for does and/or a would-be predator like a hunter. This behavior is especially true on narrow-ridge funnels. The more we hunt these types of funnels, the farther downwind we set up. Typically, we find that 30, 40 or even 50 yards is just the right distance.

Some great funnels are located near water. Lots of deer move through the shallowest part of a creek or river. If a water crossing is narrow, that's better yet. We often walk for hours along a creek or river looking for every crossing. This quick-hit tactic is a surefire way to assess hard-to-hunt deer.

Remember, the loose and moist soil types found near waterways can be deceiving when it comes to deer sign, because tracks don't disappear quickly and, therefore, it often appears more deer are using the routes. When we locate a creek crossing with big-buck tracks, we immediately determine how far deer bed and feed from that crossing. If bedding cover is close (within 400 yards), we'll set up at the funnel. If not, we'll sneak toward the bedding area and look for a staging area. These areas are magical close to the rut, because would-be suitors show up before last light, stalling until dark before proceeding toward a food source.

Hunters often overlook ponds and levees. In the right situation, both can

be a bridge for whitetails that move from one block of timber to the next. During hot and dry periods, ponds are deer magnets. Learning how whitetails use water sources is critical. We generally observe such areas for several days to establish where deer approach during various winds. We often set up with a shot to the dam or levee when the wind blows down the backside into a deep drainage. We're careful not to overhunt any water source, as deer are extremely skittish in these areas. Two to four sittings at any pond site during autumn are our maximum. Any more intrusion and you can bet they'll know somebody's there!

Also keep in mind that a funnel does not have to be a noticeable depression or hump in the ground. In the Midwest, one of our all-time favorite funnels is a point-to-point crossing in a CRP field. By studying aerial photos and glassing, we hone in on the tightest, narrowest point between two strips of cover. When crossing open

ground, lots of deer, and some big bucks, run the choke point between the two timbers, minimizing their exposure.

If it's easier for you to walk around a structure, it's easier for deer to skirt it as well. Be on the lookout for a ditch, deep slough, creek bank or the like. Then check the flat, gentle edges around it for trails and big tracks where deer skirt the obstacle. That's another great choke point and an awesome spot for a stand.

Create a funnel. We have another theory: If you build it, they will come. By creating our own funnels, we have enticed many does and some mighty fine bucks to walk within bow-range.

We have tractors on the farms we own. When clearing ground and planting food plots, we sometimes build brush piles along field and timber edges: The longer and taller the pile, the better. Because deer cannot walk through it or jump over it, they must walk around one end of it. We find that this tactic works especially well when we combine a brush pile with an existing topographical dumping ground like hog-backs or the narrow point of a ridge.

We don't just build a barrier any old place. We consider the predomi-

Dirt from a deer's hooves or a slight tuft of hair is all the proof we need that a fence jump is working.

RIGHT:
Notice the distinct
trail coming
through the grass
and onto the dam

BELOW:
The steepness of
this creek bank
keeps most of the
movement coming
up and down the
gentle slope in
the background.

nant winds in an area and then go to work. We often pile lines of brush that run straight to good trees where we like to set up. Sometimes one of those trees is downwind of a large hole we intentionally leave in a brush wall. It's another one of the tricks we took from killing that big deer along the huge windrow in Illinois.

You can also create the same type of "end around" funnel by running a long line of

round hay bales along a field or timber edge. If you don't own a tractor, ask a farmer or ranch hand to do it for you. Give him a few bucks for his trouble, and you'll have a super spot to hunt.

Timber funnels can also be created on a smaller, simpler scale.

Consider the predominant wind in an area, pick a good tree for a stand, and go to work. Drag plenty of logs, fallen treetops and brush onto an open ridge or into a flat bottom. You might even

block a major deer trail. A mature buck might walk around the barrier and into tight bow range. We generally don't use this tactic unless it's in January or February. Deer need time to get used to changes in their environment. Trying it in October or November freaks them out, trust us!

Fence jumps can be magical places to meet up with an unsuspecting trophy. Sometimes we pull down the top two or three strands of a four- or five-wire fence on the farms we own. Dirt from a deer's hoofs or hair on a wire is all the proof we need that a fence jump is working. We set up downwind.

Another great way to funnel deer is to

ABOVE:
Pond dams are often overlooked funnels yet in the right area they can be magical bridges from one structure to another.

LEFT:
If it's easier for you to walk around a ditch it will be for the deer as well. They can be very picky about their preferred travel routes.

One of the most difficult things in hunting deer is picking the exact spot amidst an endless landscape of cover and trails.

drop the gap gate of a fence and leave it open for a long time. Deer will become accustomed to walking along the fence and through the gap. If you don't own the property you're hunting, be sure to get permission from the landowner before creating a fence jump or opening a gate.

Good Access. We carefully plan access routes to and from our stands so as to disturb as few deer as possible. We are sticklers about it! We never use a flashlight in the morning, so we need a relatively clean and quiet access into each funnel.

If we're scouting a farm in January or February, we don't think twice about cutting wide, clean swaths into areas where we plan to hang stands next fall. In late summer, we might brush-hog a path from a food plot to one of our stands. Deer often walk that

cut strip, so we've created yet another funnel! We cut far less in September and October. We believe that in a high-pressure area, deer associate fresh trimming with human intrusion.

With careful planning, you will become a better hunter by taking advantage of the whitetail's key weakness: laziness. The fact that they are so reluctant to move naturally during daylight hours is the reason why funnels work. A whitetail will invariably conserve energy; it's the way they survive. Set up within range of the path of least resistance, and you can maximize your valuable time in the woods. ∎

LEFT: Our access routes to and from any stand including funnels are carefully planned out so as not to disturb any deer going in or out.

Two hog backs or ridges coming together into a drainage serve as a great dumping ground for deer movement, consistent winds are hard to achieve though in these situations.

One of our favorite stand locations is a tight, point to point crossing in this CRP field.

CHAPTER FOUR

THE BAD MOON A RISING

I t's not like Mark and I shared a hunting lease or anything with a member of the rock band Credence Clearwater Revival, but we can certainly relate to one of their classic tunes. When we see the bad moon

a rising in the afternoon, especially during the seeking phase of the pre-rut in late October or early November, we key on this like blood-thirsty coyotes. Our demeanors change. We put the serious, butt-kicking side of our game faces on. We're just more intense and focused – mentally and strategically – when the moon is right.

We put a lot of faith in a moon that rises around 1 or 2 p.m. and hangs high in the sky at 4 or 5 o'clock, which coincides with the normal travel and feeding times of whitetails. However, we also look for other important things: a high-pressure weather system; a rising barometer, preferably above 30 inches; and falling temperatures in the 35- to 45-degree range. When these conditions coexist during an evening, and that might happen only two or three times each fall, you will experience some of the best deer movement you've ever seen, guaranteed! We say

■ Each fall we're blessed with a short window of incredible buck movement known as the pre-rut's seeking phase. Some years are better than others, because the timing of lunar phases vary from year to year. However, our tactics for "shooting the moon" differ slightly from the other lunar wizards. Mark and I firmly believe the moon is one of three primary triggers that drive whitetail movement. In this chapter, we'll tell all we know and believe regarding the moon, and we'll weave that information around the bewitching tale of the oldest, heaviest buck I've ever shot.

that knowing full well there are few guarantees in whitetail hunting.

It all came together for me one enchanted evening a few years ago. It was a hunt I'll never forget. Come to think of it, it was two mystical evenings.

On Oct. 30, Mark and I crept onto one of my favorite farms. The farm is only about 80 acres, but it's a little place where deer appear comfortable feeding, meeting and mingling during the pre-rut's seeking phase. The heart of the spot is a narrow, secluded cornfield, which is rimmed by tall timbers on both sides. This field provides a staging area for deer before they reach their final destination, a 50-acre field.

It was one of those perfect afternoons when you can hike freely to your stand without breaking a sweat; when you breathe deeply the cool, crisp autumn air and are thankful you're alive and out in the timber, bow in hand. Mark and I climbed quietly to our stands on the edge of the cut corn and readied our gear. I gazed toward the sky and smiled. The faint moon shone like a big ivory cue ball.

The does arrived early, piling into the cornfield well before dark. Several young bucks hooked up with them later, skittering around like frisky teen-agers, harassing the does and nudging them here and there. It was a lively skit, and it went on till dusk.

Until he strode out into the field and stole the show.

My demeanor changed, from watching and smiling at the young deer to locking in for the kill on this monster. The muscle-bound 9-point

with incredible body girth was one of the most impressive creatures I had seen in years. He kept moving toward us, walking with the cocky, stiff-legged gait of a bodybuilder. I put tension on the bowstring as the hog stopped full frame in Mark's camera. But a big tree blocked the shot! I frantically leaned left and right, contorting in the stand to no avail. The bruiser walked on out into the middle of the field, well out of bow range. He locked in on some does and suddenly vanished into the darkness.

Dreams are made from encounters with a mature whitetail like that. Our ultimate goal is to harvest a mature buck regardless of the rack. You imprint the picture of his bull-thick body and heavy rack in your mind. The slim possibility of one day getting a bowshot at an awesome animal like that keeps bringing you back for more.

Mark departed to spend time with his daughter, Taylor, while celebrating Halloween, so our friend Steve Coon graciously helped out by running the camera. "Coon Dog" and I crept back onto the farm early the next afternoon. There's something magical and mystical about bowhunting on Oct.

31. I don't know if it's the deer gods, or the spirits, or what. I just know Halloween has been good to both Mark and I.

Little did I know this bewitching evening would top them all.

The weather remained perfect, the wind was perfect, and the moon was still up. However, I thought our stands were a little off, so we moved and tweaked the set, hoping to take that shot-blocking tree out of play. We climbed up, and the show began shortly.

A young 8-point stepped out to the edge of the field, stood tall and ogled some does that were already feeding. He proceeded to rip a scrape and hook the licking branch above it with his rack. He was feeling the inner urges of the rut and soon wandered off to sniff some does.

More does piled into the field, followed by several $2^1/_2$ - and $3^1/_2$ - year-old bucks. I studied those boys. They looked in limbo. They had come here to feed, but now, pestering the girls and pushing them around, they had other wicked things on their minds. Does are often more receptive to some bucks more than others. The high-pressure, cool weather, rising moon — the triggers — were all at work, and the deer were feeling it.

At 4:45, a big 8-point stepped out of the timber and strolled into the field, scattering does everywhere. He was well out of bow range, so emotionally it was no big deal — until I caught a flash of movement close and to my right. I peeked down and gasped. There stood a huge 10-point, a truly ancient deer. He had a cow-like stature, with a thick chest and a low-hanging belly. His muzzle was gray, and skin hung loose in wrinkles on his neck. That's the kind of fully mature buck you want to hunt. I forget all about the huge-bodied 9-point now. I put my hunt-

ing face on, I guess you could call it a Halloween mask, and locked in for the kill.

The old buck swaggered into shooting range and posed for Coon Dog's camera. I put tension on the bowstring and just about came unglued. Was this an evil Halloween trick? Just like the big 9-point the afternoon before, this buck was parked behind a tree. I had no shot! The deer put his head down and strode toward the middle of the cornfield.

I'm sure dejection would have set in any minute, but there was no time for that. Across the field and coming out the far timber was another tall-racked shooter!

"Man, this is unbelievable," Coon Dog whispered, his camera whirring and burning tape.

"What an evening," I agreed. "I've never seen so many thumpers in one spot in my life!"

The last big deer strolled to the far end of the field, doing his limbo thing, crunching corn and nudging does, as dusk seeped in all around and chilled the timber a few more degrees. My spirits were going the way of the coming gloom. I sighed and pulled down my facemask, thinking it was all over for the day. Oh well, I knew I had just experienced one of the greatest evenings ever. Thankful just to be a part of it, I peeked out into the field one last time.

I gasped as I spotted another huge buck, angling straight toward us!

I grabbed my bow and looked closer. My heart jumped and my knees almost buckled. It was the muscle-bound 9-point from the day before! He kept coming and cruised by at 37 steps. That's farther than I like to shoot at a buck given my druthers, but I was confident I could pull off the shot.

I drew my bow and grunted. The deer kept walking. Frantically, I grunted again, then again, cranking up the volume of each call. The last one caught his attention. The instant his hoofs froze, I settled in and let it fly. It was if time stood still for a few seconds. I'll never forget the sight of that arrow plunking home just behind the

buck's front leg, low in the lungs and heart. The white-dipped arrow and white fletching flew like a dart, burning a lasting impression in my mind.

The buck wheeled and bounded off into the timber. "There! I just heard him crash down, thank God!" I yelled.

I looked up at Coon Dog. He was more rattled than I, mumbling, "Oh baby, you got him Terry, you got him, you got him." I'll never forget that look on my friend's face. I tried to settle him down, not an easy chore because I too was shaking.

It was one of my best bowshots ever, and the buck didn't go far. When we found him in a deep ravine, my first impression was, "His

rack is nice, but his body is gargantuan, even bigger than I thought." He had the rough, thick look of an old deer. I figure he was at least 5 ½ years old, or older. When bucks reach full maturity, their age becomes difficult to determine.

It was pitch dark now. The bad moon had risen to cast an eerie, amber glow over the still timber. The silence was deafening. Indeed, there was something mystical in the air that night. How Coon Dog and I got the huge buck out of there I still don't know. The deer activity was so hot in that area that we didn't want to lure in any coyotes, so we dragged the beast out without gutting him. How we muscled the hog up into the bed of my truck is still a mystery. I vividly recall the bed liner slipping beneath our feet as we made several attempts to hoist him into the back.

The next day, we drove the buck to a meat locker and weighed

him. The deer was field-dressed now, and he bottomed out the hanging scales at 220 pounds! I reckon he weighed 230 or 240 pounds dressed, which would put him well over 275 on the hoof. He was the oldest, heaviest buck I have ever shot. The painstaking task of loading and unloading him in and out of the truck for photos and the like became a labor of love — a Halloween treat that to this day tops them all.

LESSONS
LEARNED

The Rising and Falling Moon. One of the most prominent lessons we've learned over the years is that the best ruts occur, at least here in the Midwest, when the weather is cool and the moon rises in late October or early November. This is the seeking phase of the pre-rut, and a rising moon around 4 or 5 p.m. puts a lot of does on their feet

"I see the bad moon arising."

and moves them early and hard toward food sources. In turn, this drives bucks, which are now feeling the first surges of testosterone, toward the food sources, where they go from doe to doe, trying to nudge out the first hot one. My hunt for the 9-point beast illustrates that to a tee.

On the flip side, a falling moon occurs sometime shortly after a rising-moon. That's when Mark and I switch gears and hunt hard during mornings, trying to catch deer on their way back to their beds. When a falling moon occurs during the first two hours of daylight, we typically see a lot of deer moving in funnels and along the edges of bedding areas.

We don't believe the moon necessarily triggers the peak of the rut. We have learned that here in the Midwest the rut hits around the same time each year, sometime between Nov. 5 and 20. Whether the bulk of rut activity happens at night or during daylight depends on whether the moon is rising or falling during certain phases of the breeding season. So, depending on when the moon rises and falls each autumn, it exposes different parts of the rut. Things are different every year, but our hunting is invariably best when a rising or falling moon overlaps the seeking phase in late October or early November. Be conscious of that and try to hunt hard when it happens.

Although we focus on the moon during the rut, we also work it into our plans early and late in the season. Mark and I have so much faith in our lunar technique that we now plan our out-of-state bowhunts in September and

ABOVE: Nothing gets us more excited then knowing the moon is on the rise when we strap up and head into an afternoon stand.

RIGHT: It's the stories shared after the hunt that we all remember years later

October around the rising moon. Early in the season, the best hunting occurs around food sources in the afternoons, so we try to gain every advantage, like the rising moon putting deer on their feet and driving them toward the feed earlier than normal. Sometimes, if we can't schedule a hunt during a good moon time, we don't waste our time and money traveling out of state.

We never overlook December. When the weather cools and a rising moon returns and triggers deer movement, the late season is an awesome time. In fact, we view it as one of the best times of the season to kill a mature buck on or near a food source. Just look at a buck's physiology. He's trying to rebuild fat reserves he used while fighting other bucks and chasing and breeding does. Suddenly, the rising moon returns in early, mid or late December. It doesn't matter. When it happens, hungry bucks move hard toward crop fields and usually well before sunset. In these instances, Mark and I stake out a field and watch for the big boys.

LEFT: We've used many tags during an afternoon rising moon or a morning falling moon.

BELOW: Some of the best footage in our 15-year history comes under optimum moon conditions

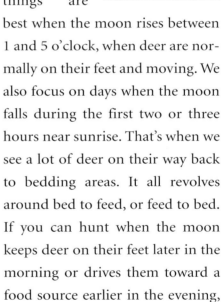

Keep An Eye on the Moon. To determine precisely when the moon is rising or falling, we go to the U.S. Naval Observatory's Web site and study moonrise and moonset times. Type in your hunting area, click "search," and the chart tells you, in military time, when the moon rises and sets each day during hunting season.

We focus on those nine or 10 days each month when the moon rises in the afternoon. We've found things are best when the moon rises between 1 and 5 o'clock, when deer are normally on their feet and moving. We also focus on days when the moon falls during the first two or three hours near sunrise. That's when we see a lot of deer on their way back to bedding areas. It all revolves around bed to feed, or feed to bed. If you can hunt when the moon keeps deer on their feet later in the morning or drives them toward a food source earlier in the evening, you've got the best odds of shooting a buck.

We also monitor the moon as it rises later each afternoon. Note

Clouds or not;
the moon still
affects when and
how deer move.

ABOVE: Terry and Steve "Coon Dog" with Terry's monster.

RIGHT: Add a rising moon to an approaching cold front and the results might scare you at food sources.

the time when you see the first deer enter a food source. On subsequent days, deer are apt to show up later, until finally you see no afternoon movement. Mark and I believe this happens because the moon is rising later each day.

We keep tabs on the moon when we're shooting our bows in June, July, August and September.

If you're outside practicing in the morning, say 7:30 or 8 a.m., make a mental note if the moon is still up and shining faintly in the sky. I often jot it down in a daily log. If the moon is still up at 8 a.m. on Aug. 15, for example, it will be up around 8 a.m. within a few days of Sept. 15. It's pretty much the same deal in the afternoon. If you're shooting your bow and the moon's still up at 3:30 or 4:30 p.m., you can bet the following month, within a day or so, the moon will be up at about the same time. Over the summer, we monitor the moon and predict when we should see the best deer movement in October, November and December. You should, too.

Even in intensely pressured areas we've observed the moon having a huge affect.

Remember the Other Buck Triggers. We believe the moon is one of three primary factors that directly affect how and when whitetails move throughout fall. That said, we also believe the big orb is the weakest link.

Weather and the rut are by far the main triggers of deer movement. We find activity is best on high-pressure days with a rising barometer, preferably above 30 inches, and cool temperatures in the 35- to 45-degree range. And then there's the rut. Nothing puts big deer on their feet like the uncontrollable urge to breed does.

RIGHT: Even our calling seems to work better during favorable moon times.

BELOW: We hang a lot of stands in January and February anticipating next falls rising moons.

❧

Years ago, Mark and I would sit and hunt, not really understanding why we weren't seeing any deer some days. We're analytical, painstakingly so, so we just had to find out. We analyzed all sorts of things and came up with three big reasons. Of course, you've got to have food sources and good cover, but if you focus on our three main triggers, we believe you can predict when hunting is going to be its best. When it all comes together — cool, high-pressure during the seeking phase of the pre-rut with the moon

LEFT: Our confidence soars when certain weather, rut and moon cycles coincide. Our history shows incredible success rates when all three triggers align.

BELOW: When the moon is right our videoing, photography and hunting success all soar.

rising or falling — we think your chances of seeing and killing a mature buck are excellent. So look at the big picture and key in on all three triggers:

1. Weather.
2. Rut.
3. Moon. ■

ABOVE: A falling moon in the a.m. puts us close to security cover.

RIGHT: Keeping your eye on the moon times can put you in the right place at the right time.

CHAPTER FIVE

BEAT THEM
TO BED

One clear, brisk November day, Mark and I, along with our friend Steve Stoltz checked one of our favorite spots in Illinois. It was one of those little gems that hold huge bucks in these modern times. The 53-acre tract consisted of 20 acres of crops, 20 acres of timber and 13 acres of CRP ground. That diversity is what draws and holds whitetails. Because we were new to the property, we were unfamiliar with regular travel patterns. Of particular interest to me was a long, narrow hollow that ran east-west in the timber.

Mark and Steve were jovial and chattered about everything under the sun as we poked around, glassing for deer and snooping for sign. I was serious as a brain surgeon. Mark and I needed a spot to hunt and film the next few weeks, and it was our job to dissect the terrain. Somehow over the years I've become the designated strategist of the Drury morning hunt. However, I relish the challenge of homing in on spots to ambush giant bucks in the glimmering pink of dawn on their way back to bed. Mark, on the other hand, is the grand master of the evening assault. We have contrasting styles, but we're extremely effective when working in tandem.

We don't like to penetrate cover often, especially thick bedding areas, so I worked the edges of the brushy hollow, scouting from the

■ As white-tailed bucks mature from age $3\frac{1}{2}$ to $5\frac{1}{2}$, they acquire more nocturnal tendencies. The window of morning movement can sometimes be extremely short and tenuous to hunt. This chapter highlights a quick but intense dawn hunt for a gnarly, old 8-point. Mark and I reveal our meticulously planned and executed methods for cutting off bucks en route to their bedrooms.

outside in. The sign was there, heavy and smoking-hot on the fringes. Six- to eight-inch cedars had been ripped from stem to stern; the big rubs oozed sap and shined like beacons. A line of dank, moist, musky scrapes wound back toward the heart of the draw. The tractor tire-size ovals were pocked with wide, blocky tracks. At least one good buck was working the hollow and likely bedding in there, and I had a hunch where to hunt him.

"Over here," I whispered to Mark and Steve as I headed to the head of the hollow on the northwestern corner of the property. According to the Weather Channel, the wind would stay out of the southeast the next few mornings. If we hung our stands here, we might catch a buck moving up over the ridge into the hollow from the crop fields below, approaching from the west to scent-check the entire draw, mostly for does but also for other bucks and danger, before slipping into the cover. The distinct scrape line that ran from west to east down the center of the deep hollow can easily be inspected with one small gust of an easterly wind. In early November, we've observed many mature bucks do just that before committing to their desired route in search of the first estrous doe. One undetectable odor at 250 to 300 yards can turn a buck on a dime and send him in the opposite direction.

I waved my hands toward a straight tree and said, "Right there, boys." Now, try and imagine three accomplished whitetail hunters agreeing on the same tree to hunt from. Well, that just wasn't happening, but I won the debate after several minutes of rebuttals.

"Whatever," Mark said as we went to work. He might have sounded nonchalant, but I knew he was OK with my plan. When it comes to hanging a morning set, Mark has come to trust his older brother's judgment unequivocally. We hung two stands in minutes, trimmed several shooting lanes and bade Steve farewell and good luck for the next morning. We then headed back to camp. I had aerial photos and maps to scour, and I wanted to check the Weather

Channel for the umpteenth time to make sure I got all the details. We had hunted the farm and the hollow previously, but when you're after a mature, mega whitetail, you leave no stone unturned.

A zillion stars blinked overhead as we sneaked toward the hollow the next morning. We crept in from the south, skirting the edge of a low-lying crop field, having learned from past observation that several whitetails linger and move there in the pre-dawn darkness. We crossed a deep ditch and began the long, steep hike up a hill on the far western edge of the property. We walked parallel to a wire fence, using brush and a strip of inordinately tall weeds to cover our approach. At least the going was quiet. In summer, we hiked in there and mowed an access strip along the western edge of the timber, just in case we needed to sneak in there on a southeast wind during hunting season.

Although we packed our heavy jackets, we began sweating midway up the hill, perspiring lightly at first, until streams poured down our faces. You never want to sweat and stink up the joint on the hike into a stand, knowing full well the shivers that are to come once the sun rises and temperatures drop a few degrees. But it happens. We pressed on.

Finally we reached the top, huffing and puffing and blowing plumes of steam into the chilly air. Our hearts pounded like tiny jackhammers, not only from the hike but

also at the prospects of the hunt to come. Huge bucks lurked in the area, but we had to hustle. Gray, dingy light was seeping into the hollow, and with the long walk we were running behind schedule.

We spotted our landmark, a towering brush pile on the northern tip of the farm. The landowner had made it with a bulldozer while installing a new wire fence months earlier.

We eased toward the brush pile, shimmied over it and took great pains not to snap a single stick. We slipped out the far side and through the last patch of multi-flora rose – avoiding the briars in front of our faces – before hitting the edge of the hollow. Whew, we finally made it!

We Spidermanned up the tree, Mark first, because he was filming. We secured our safety harnesses and readied our gear, being careful not to clang a bow limb or a camera brace against the side

of a steel stand. Having just secured my release aid, I was about two minutes from being fully ready when I heard Mark.

"Oooopp, Terry there's a buck." I'd know that familiar tone anywhere. Brother Mark had spotted a big deer.

My eyes nearly popped out of my head as I frantically scanned

the hollow. Mark's low-light vision is incredible. Sometimes I think he can see as well or better than a whitetail in the twilight, a God-given talent that I wish I had.

"AAAAGGH! Is that him?" I hissed, spotting movement that I soon identified as the monster buck.

He was an old deer, chunky and thick-necked, with a short, blocky face and light-colored hair around his sagging eye sockets. I sure didn't need to peek at his rack to know he was a shooter, but who can resist? "Oh, man!" I gasped again. He was one of those gnarly 8-points with incredible mass. And he was right there, 30 yards away and boring straight for us!

In a pressure cooker like that you don't act, you react. Going on pure instinct and adrenaline, I grabbed my bow, locked in on the thick deer's shoulder and drew. I never heard Mark hiss, "No, no, no," as I grunted, stopped the monster at 10 steps, and let the arrow fly.

I was pumped and ecstatic – until I turned, looked up into the camera and saw the bland look on my brother's face.

"Oh no, what's wrong?" I asked.

"Nothing's wrong, you hit him

good," Mark replied. "From my angle, he was smack behind a big tree when you shot. But don't worry, it will still make a great hunt."

I must confess to being bummed. It's the fine emotional line you walk in our business. The hunter in you wants to shoot a huge buck the second you get the opportunity. But we obviously want our video kills to be awesome, tight and full frame. In this case, Mark had done his job, spotting the big boy and filming him all the way in. I, on the other hand, had jumped the gun.

But you know what? That happens when a giant deer rambles in and catches you by surprise. We

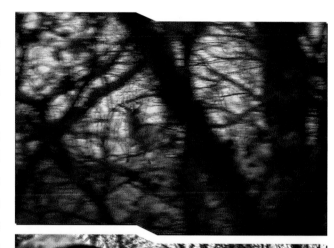

hadn't been up that tree 10 minutes. The pink sun was peeking its gorgeous head up in the east, and we had a dream buck out there on the ground somewhere. We had made it happen. Mark is a wizard at building and editing our hunts, and whenever he says

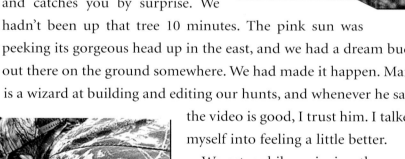

the video is good, I trust him. I talked myself into feeling a little better.

We sat awhile, enjoying the spectacular sunrise and the sounds of nature awakening one more time. We've seen those sights and heard those sounds hundreds of times, but they never get old.

Mark broke the silence. "You

know, Terry, we walked right past that bruiser. He was somewhere between here and the ag-field down in the bottom that we skirted. Man, he was right there in that patch of timber, and somehow we slipped past him. And we got him!"

I was feeling a lot better now. Once again, our meticulous planning paid off. Careful access on an easterly wind paid big dividends.

Now all that was left was to find the buck. Much to our chagrin, he bolted out of the hollow, crossed a pasture and disappeared onto the next property. That happens sometimes when you hunt a small tract, and you should always do the right thing. Mark and I left, visited the neighbor and got his permission to recover our trophy. We returned, huffed, puffed and sweated our way back up the hill and made a beeline for the point of impact.

"Man, I don't think I've ever seen an arrow covered with more blood," I said to Mark as I examined the shaft. There were tufts of hair all around and sprays of blood where the buck ran off. Smiling, we inched ahead, searching for the buck that we knew lay just ahead.

However, an hour later, we were on our hands and knees dissecting dirt and leaves for specks of blood the size of pinheads. Our cockiness and confidence had spiraled steadily down to the depths of trepidation. How could this be happening? How had the buck come this far – I thought I double-lunged him? Will we find him? The mind games began, and I berated myself for jumping the gun. We didn't have the luxury of rewinding the tape and reviewing and analyzing the hit like we normally do. However, I relived the shot many times in my mind, and I couldn't understand how he could go so far.

We did have one thing going for us. The buck had run off to the east and south, so we were able to keep the wind pretty much in our faces as we crawled and searched and hoped. We moved slowly and talked in whispers so as not to jump the buck out of his bed.

On we went. The sun kept getting higher, and the day was warming nicely, although I hardly noticed it in my anxiety. Mark stood up, flexed his back to work the kinks out, and suddenly screeched, "There he is!"

The fact the adrenaline-driven deer had gone almost 400 yards and been a bear to find was lost on me now. This was one gorgeous critter, in a gnarly sort of way. He just oozed maturity — the incredible girth of his body, the thick, coarse coat,

the Angus-like neck, the blocky face, the narrow-slit eyes, and the massive, clubby 153-inch rack. He was at least $5\frac{1}{2}$ years old. Mark and I will undoubtedly kill more bucks with our beat-them-to-bed strategy. But I can't imagine shooting one with more darn character.

BILL MARCHEL

LESSONS LEARNED

Mornings vs. Evenings. Sometimes Mark and I think and act a lot alike. But people who have spent much time around us know full well we can be like oil and water. We just don't agree on some things, and we're not shy to let each other know it. Sometimes it gets pretty darn heated and loud as we express our admittedly hard-headed opinions. I guess it's just that brotherly thing.

We certainly have different views on morning versus evening hunting. Mark concentrates on afternoon setups near food sources. I often call brother Mark the mad scientist because he has become so wickedly consumed with food plots. Most people plant clover and crops and then set their tree stands accordingly. Well, Mark spends days, weeks, sometimes even years picking out the right trees for our stands. Then he plants corn, soybeans or Biologic around the trees, creating funnels, edges and inside corners where we can cut off bucks on their way to the feed. I must admit it's pretty amazing to watch him think and work.

As for me, I concentrate on morning setups. I'm forever focusing on timber edges, brushy fringes,

Our access routes to and from every stand are carefully planned so as not to spook any deer.

RIGHT:
Usually by sunrise we will have been in our stands for at least an hour.

BELOW:
During gun season we like to still hunt our way into the stand, during legal shooting hours.

narrow hollows, hogbacks and other spots where we can slip in unannounced, hang stands near "sacred grounds" and ambush bucks at first light. The bottom line is that Mark is far better than I at picking a spot for an evening stand. But I've got him hands down when it comes to hanging morning stands.

We didn't plan it that way. The morning/evening thing just evolved over the years, and it's been great for our hunting. By having the two different concepts, we talk, agree, argue, yell and cuss about why to hunt a partic-

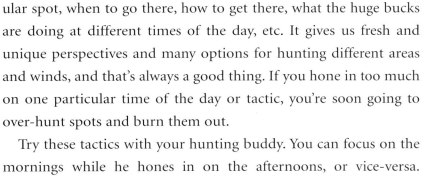

ular spot, when to go there, how to get there, what the huge bucks are doing at different times of the day, etc. It gives us fresh and unique perspectives and many options for hunting different areas and winds, and that's always a good thing. If you hone in too much on one particular time of the day or tactic, you're soon going to over-hunt spots and burn them out.

Try these tactics with your hunting buddy. You can focus on the mornings while he hones in on the afternoons, or vice-versa. Bounce your thoughts and ideas off each other and agree to disagree on occasion. It sounds weird, but you'll become better hunters.

Stay tuned, because Mark offers many tips on afternoon hunting near food sources, especially in Chapter 9. Here, because we're concentrating on morning hunts, I'd like to make a major point about deer behavior near bedding areas.

Many hunters overlook the facts that mature bucks skulk and scent-check "sacred ground" before they commit to it. But it's

A heavy-horned 8-point Terry beat to bed in 1999.

Our good friend
Steve Stoltz waited
until 9:30 one
November morning
before a hot doe
drug this 160-inch
10-point into a
known bedding
area.

something we've observed many times over the past 20 years, especially over the past 10 to 12 years of videoing hunts. It has caused us to incorporate three simple "got to" rules into our morning hunting repertoire:

1. You've got to carefully monitor wind direction and speed each and every morning, making sure it blows out from a bedding area to you. Be fully aware and always conscious of your thermals.

2. You've got to access a stand from a downwind position and then set up 100 to 150 yards downwind of a bedding area, and

3. You've got to be there and set up, quickly and quietly – the earlier the better –

LEFT: Sometimes distant morning observation helps us determine the correct access route.

BELOW: When any deer approaches we're fanatical about being ready and not moving. Movement on stand is a huge problem for hunters.

ABOVE: We often glass a known feed field in the pre-dawn before crossing it to a stand. We will not go farther until it is clear. Don't spook the deer you're hunting.

RIGHT: Cattle pastures are great means of access for morning stands.

before an old buck comes by to scent-check the cover before he enters it, you are alert and ready.

Access is the key. One thing we've learned over the years is that how you get to a tree stand is 50 percent of the game. On second thought, when trying to beat a mature buck back to his morning bed, smart access is 90 percent of the game! Particularly in early November during the pre-rut when bucks begin the seeking phase. They tend to roam more in search of hot does, but they still faithfully return to their normal havens.

Mark and I wouldn't have had a snowball's chance in hell at that gnarly 8-point had we not meticulously planned our approach, played the southeast wind, slipped along the western edge of the property, climbed the steep hill silently and used brush, weeds and structure to cover our moves. The buck was right there, probably less than 150 yards away and moving toward his bedding area, when we climbed to our set. Thanks to a little luck and a lot of careful planning, we were able to squeeze in there and kill him.

That planning begins with countless hours of observation, as we talked about in Chapter 2. Before you move in and hunt tight to a bedding area, you ought to set up 400 yards or so off the cover and observe deer for at least several mornings, if not a week or a month. Remember our mantra: Observe more and hunt less for more success.

At first light, glass field edges, timber edges, fencerows, ditches, creek bottoms, brushy funnels — any travel routes does and bucks use when returning from a food source to a sacred ground. Make detailed notes of the wind direction and speed. Some patterns will soon emerge. Cross-reference the deer sightings against the terrain and cover of an aerial photograph. Then hurry up and wait some more for perfect conditions. Hunting close to a bedding area is risky business. We generally don't move in until we get cool weather and high pressure (we covered that in Chapter 1) and we like for the moon to be falling in the morning, as mentioned in Chapter 4.

Shed antlers in the spring are wonderful bed-room markers. Every clue a buck gives you must be calculated.

The first calling series in the morning are often our most effective.

When we go in, it's generally early, in the wee hours of the pre-dawn. Because of the long, steep walk to the hollow, we were running late on the hunt for the 153-inch buck. We still got him, but there was admittedly some luck involved. Had we been 10 minutes later, we probably would have bumped that deer, or he would have been past us and already in bed when we climbed to our stands. There's another lesson: Get there early. Try to be in your stand and settled an hour before the pink sunrise.

I should note that when

Mark and I are running late, we feverishly glass fields, edges and timber openings as we sneak. If we spot a single doe or buck, we stop and don't take another step until the coast is clear. If you spook just one deer and it blows and crashes into a bedding area, it will alert every deer in the sanctuary.

If you're like us, you want everything just right.

A majority of the hunts on our first two videos were in the morning.

Be as quiet as a mouse. Sneak quickly and fluidly across a pasture or field where past observation told you deer travel in the morning. If possible, take a mower and make a walking strip to your stand in summer. Clear the path of all debris. This will pay huge dividends during hunting season.

Use cover to your advantage when slipping toward a stand. Tall weeds, thickets, cedar or pine trees, and briers along the edge of a field … you get the picture. Think about clipping a clear, quiet path through the brush and close to your stand before the season.

LEFT: Todd Smith shot a beautiful 8-point in one of our best security cover stands.

Use structure for concealment. Hide in ditches or steep creek drainages. We have a lot of those here in the Midwest, and we use them a lot. Hide behind a string of big round hay bales, the backside of a hogback, a linear brush pile or wind break … again, you get the idea.

Wind direction is obviously crucial. It must be blowing straight out of a bedding cover and into your face, or quartering out of a sacred ground and blowing your scent away from a travel route where deer will slip in downwind. Don't risk it if the wind is wrong or even marginal.

When possible plan your approach to a stand so the wind is right all the way in. That's what Mark and I did on the hunt for the 153-inch giant. We came in from the south, walked the western edge of

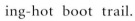

the property until we reached the northern tip, then turned and angled into the hollow from northwest. The southeast wind was perfect all the way to our stand. Furthermore, we hid behind cover and structure all the way. Deer could neither smell nor see us, and that's always what you want.

But it's tricky. Remember, just like you, a mature buck is working his way toward a bedding area from either downwind or quartering with the wind at his rear during first light. You obviously don't want to bump into him, or let him cut your smoking-hot boot trail.

Here's where observation comes in big time. Say one morning you have a cool northwest wind. You have spotted a good buck circling into a dense thicket from the southeast. Plan your approach from the northeast or due east to avoid an ugly and hunt-ruining confrontation with the big deer.

On farms 400 to 500 acres or larger, Mark and I typically plan our approaches to a sacred ground in a roundabout way, sometimes making a big loop and cutting in toward the cover from downwind. But on a small tract, like the 53-acre hollow where I killed the big boy, we are often forced by the property lines to walk extremely tight to bedding cover. When you're in

A huge 163-inch buck shot by Brad Rucks just after first light.

that situation, just do your best. Go in downwind, sneak in early and quietly and hide as best you can. Under the cover of darkness a buck might tolerate some noise, but it certainly will not tolerate your scent. With luck, you can slip in tight and practically climb into bed with a giant buck.

Expandable Broadheads are the Answer. During our hunt for the 153-inch buck, we were still shooting fixed-blade broadheads. For us it was a pretty typical fixed-blade track job, even though the shot double-lunged him. It was a nerve-racking, get-on-your-hands-and-knees-and-crawl effort that spanned 350 to 400 yards. We are still awestruck at the amazing will to live that mature whitetails possess. However, we cannot stress enough the importance of an accurate shot within the vitals for a clean effective harvest.

Since then we have switched exclusively to expandable broadheads. I shoot a Spitfire with a 1¹/₂-inch cutting diameter, and Mark uses the 1¹/₂-inch Rocket Sidewinder. In our opinion a 1¹/₂-inch cutting diameter is the minimum you should shoot for whitetails. With a bow and arrow, you kill a deer by hemorrhage, and we've found that a razor-sharp expandable broadhead with a big cutting diameter performs best. Since we started shooting expandables — we prefer to take broadside or slightly quarter-

POSTSCRIPT

Ten days later, my son, Matt, shot his first buck with a bow, a 130-class 8-point, during a morning hunt from an evening stand. If there's a lesson to be learned, it's that if you scout, plan meticulously and choose the right tree, sometimes a spot can pay off either morning or afternoon, depending on the lay of the land and location of food sources and bedding cover. But let me push strategy aside for a moment. The fact that father and son shot a pair of Pope & Young bucks out of the same hollow in the span of 10 days is what made that deer season one to remember. The feelings of joy and pride you get when hunting with a son or daughter is indescribable.

ing-away shots — our lives have changed. Blood trails are extremely heavy and profuse, and our recovery ratio on whitetails has soared. To us, expandable broadheads are the answer. However, we realize they might not be for everyone. There will always be debates in bowhunting: expandable vs. fixed; carbon vs. aluminum; compound vs. recurve, etc. Choose what works best for you and shoot with extreme confidence. ■

CHAPTER SIX

∽

GROUND
ATTACK

The only weakness in our defensive armor had struck once again. We rolled out of bed late on a spectacular morning. After a string of poor-weather days with variable winds, the mercury hovered around 20 degrees, and a heavy frost coated the ground, glittering like tiny diamonds in the growing light. Even better, it was Nov. 17, the talking heads on the Weather Channel predicted a high-pressure, bluebird day, and the rut was going full tilt. And we were running late!

The pink sun inched over the horizon as Mark and I jumped into my truck and roared away on the 30-minute ride to our hunting area. We peeked through a melting patch in the frosty windshield and smiled. At least the moon, almost full, was still up and fairly high in the sky. When we're running late in the morning, there's no better feeling than to look up and see that big, beautiful moon still shining like a soft-white light bulb. Maybe that moon and the cold, high-pressure conditions would keep deer on their feet and moving a few hours after sunrise.

We'd soon find out.

▥ Not every bowhunt has to take place with the hunter perched high above the forest floor. In fact, situations and conditions often warrant a defined ground attack. That point was driven home to us one November morning a few years ago. The weather was perfect, the bucks were rutting hard, and we were late getting to our tree stands. Thank goodness! Mark and I embarked on a no-holds-barred ground mission, and we rattled in and killed a wide, massive 8-point. Since then, we often use the same down-and-dirty tactics that came to us by happenstance that wild, frosty day.

I burned up the pavement to get to our spot. We hopped out of the truck, threw our gear together and got ready to make a mad dash to our tree stands. Wait! Five bucks were dogging a doe out in the CRP field we were fixing to walk across! We scrambled for our

binoculars and soon realized two more bucks followed a doe into a small patch of timber to our left. Bucks were running everywhere!

We observed the fantastic show, totally amazed and with more than a little disbelief. I whispered to Mark, "Now this is what the rut is supposed to be like. Those bucks are rutted up something fierce this morning!" We kept watching through our binoculars and identified two bona fide shooters in the group of five bucks.

Now what?

The conversation over a makeshift strategy became heated and nearly inaudible. Mark had definite thoughts on where to go and how to approach the bucks. I had my own ideas, and I certainly wasn't shy to voice them. We hissed and moaned and spat stuff out too quickly for each other to comprehend. We finally stopped the gib-

berish and stared at each other, the looks on our faces saying, "Chill!" We gained our composure and mapped out a strategy.

The five bucks had since vanished into a brushy ravine on one edge of the CRP field. Shortly thereafter, the doe popped out and one thick-necked shooter and two of the

small bucks pushed her across the field and into a block of timber to the west. The other shooter and one of the little bucks stayed in the ravine. Now was our chance to make a break for it. We decided to sneak toward the ravine and then, if we made it, we would try to rattle in hopes of luring the lone shooter out of his security cover.

The brisk wind was perfect – blowing from the big buck to us. We might get a shot at him if we got lucky. And that was a mighty big "if." We seriously doubted things would work out as planned. We had never rattled in and killed a buck with a bow on the ground before. Come to think of it, we had never shot a buck with our bows from ground zero, period. We didn't have the security of the tree stands that we had hunted from for years, and that made us antsy and unsure of ourselves. But you know what? The deer hunter who is never willing to take a chance is doomed to failure.

We said "what the heck," and went for it.

Mark's camera rolled as we scurried across the slightly tangled CRP field. You would have roared with laughter had you seen us. We looked like a pair of overgrown ground-

hogs waddling across the frosty terrain. We paused several times to glass, then scooted to the head of the draw without spooking any deer.

So far, so good.

We set up in a narrow ditch, facing upwind, and made sure we had plenty of cover at our backs. When you hunt from the ground, thick grass or trees behind you are what breaks your hulking silhouette and helps cover your moves. I pulled out my rattling antlers

and cracked them together for about 20 seconds. I followed that up with a couple of grunts. The calls rang out in the still air. To this day, I can't believe what happened next.

I had just put down the antlers and grabbed my bow when the wildeyed 8-point popped out of the cover and trotted up the other side of the ditch, coming straight toward us! We were shocked. Mark and I had hoped for the best, but we hadn't expected this. The thick-necked buck rolled in, steam shooting from his nostrils, and stopped broadside in a wide-open spot 15 yards away. There was no time to think, and just barely enough time to react.

Going on instinct, I came to full draw and prepared to anchor, only to be blinded by the white-hot rays of the rising sun. Frantically trying to settle in behind the buck's shoulder, I had to raise the sight pins clear over the top of his back to gain a full sight picture. I slowly lowered the bow, settled the pin on

the backlit buck and readied for the shot. Through it all, I could only imagine the trouble Mark must be having. The action was fast and furious, and I knew trying to film the buck straight into the blinding sun must have been incredibly tough.

I vividly recall the next two or three seconds; they seemed to take an eternity. It was as if time slowed down just long enough for me to squeeze the release and make an accurate shot. The arrow hit home, and the buck wheeled and bounded up and over a small rise. We gave a little jubilation war cry. But mostly we just sat there stunned, looking at each other and smiling, still not really believing what had just transpired.

The shot had looked and felt good, so we started tracking. We found good blood and hair here and there and pressed on. About 250 yards later, I became concerned. We came to a fence and found where the buck had jumped it and disappeared into a small, patch of timber. Our decision was a no-brainer. We didn't want to push on and possibly bump the buck, so we backed out. That's a tough decision for any deer hunter, but it's the best option.

We returned to our motel room, grabbed some breakfast and changed into lighter clothes. It had turned out to be a spectacular day, but I was anxious and couldn't really enjoy it. Five hours later, I couldn't stand it any longer. We retuned to our hunting spot and practically ran to the fence. After crossing the fence, I knelt and found more blood and hair. I looked up and spotted the buck lying dead 25 yards away! He died within 15 to 20 seconds of the actual hit, but was rutted up enough for the adrenaline to take him a little farther than we thought he would go.

He was long of body and thick-necked, and his heavy 8-point rack scored 130. He was not the biggest buck I had ever shot, but he was one of my best for several reasons — our oversleeping, the ground assault, the rattling, the fast and furious action and the in-your-face bowshot. You never forget hunts like that.

Mark and I are low-impact hunters, and we never use an ATV to access our hunting spots. However, this buck had gone about 275 yards after the shot, and our truck was even farther than that, so we broke our rule and retrieved the four-wheeler to pack him out.

After loading up, we headed back to the motel for a little celebration and much-needed relaxation. That evening, our friends Steve Stoltz and Stan Potts stopped by, and we all watched the video again and again, relishing this unbelievable hunt.

That's when it struck me. After all these years in the video production business, I dare say that's some of our best footage ever. I still love seeing the wild-eyed buck charging in from the right. I can still feel the disbelief of it all and the anxiety of drawing my bow in his face. The buck stops broadside and blows steam just 15 yards away … the lightning-fast shot … the deer wheels and bounds away. It's all still clear as a bell in mind. My hat went off to brother Mark for his fantastic videography that wild November morning, and it remains off to this day.

LESSONS
LEARNED

Take a Chance. Don't be afraid to embark on a pointed ground attack. Mature bucks are smart! That's why there never seems to be a stand-worthy tree within bow or gun range of a field edge, crossing or funnel where you know a big buck prefers to walk. Or, you might find what looks to be a good tree for a stand only to realize the wind, visibility or shooting lanes are poor. If you're running late, don't panic. Instead, chill out, survey the situation, put the wind in your face and

still-hunt toward your spot, hiding behind cover and terrain wrinkles. Stop frequently and glass for deer. If you spot a good buck, think quickly and make a move. Your ground assault might pay off big time, like it did for Mark and I that frosty November morning.

Actually, we find that a hunter is usually better off on the ground than trying to get by in a marginal tree stand. Once the leaves fall, trees become mighty open, and it becomes increasingly difficult to hide at 20 feet off the ground. It's easier to conceal a hunter, and in our case a cameraman and his extra gear, on the ground than up a tree.

Many hunters worry too much about their scent when hunting

from the ground. If you set up right, you'll be in excellent shape. On the ground, your scent doesn't travel as far, swirl as much or disperse and pool as widely as it does from a tree stand, so fewer whitetails might actually smell you. A down-and-dirty assault can be especially good for an evening hunt. It's no big deal when the air cools and sinks, and thermals drive your scent down toward the ground, because you're already there.

Ten years ago we wouldn't have said this. But today, as Mark and I experience more ground-hunting success, we constantly look for spots that would work nicely for a surprise attack. If we nail down the movements of a big deer through long-range observation, we don't think twice about sneaking to a tall patch of weeds, switch grass, cedars or pines. Large hay bales on or near field edges are also great spots for a quick-strike ambush.

Depending on terrain and/or deer patterns, a natural blind is the

Sometimes our stands are so far in an ATV is necessary to get deer out. We never use them for access though!

best setup for a ground assault. A tall, thick fencerow or a brush pile can provide a good backdrop for erecting a blind. One of our favorite tactics is to build a cedar nest next to a large cedar tree. Keep the profile of any blind small and sleek so it blends with the terrain. We typically build ground blinds well before hunting season so deer can get used to them.

The key to any ground setup is thick, tight background cover. You can get away with little or no cover in front of you, but you'd better cover your back. A good backdrop, with few holes in it, is what hides your silhouette and covers your moves.

An erected blind where no tree exists. We gun hunt from the top and bow hunt from the lower cedar blind. This is an awesome crossing for huge bucks and it is perfect for a northwest wind.

We keep our movements to a minimum, and deer rarely see us. When a huge buck strolls within 20 yards, you must think quickly and draw your bow at the optimum time. Wait for the buck to look directly away from you or back over his shoulder.

Although we bowhunt more and move from the ground these days, gun season more often finds us moving in for a surprise. Hunting with a slug gun or a muzzleloader late in the season, we love to get down and dirty, where we can see and shoot a long way across a field or funnel.

Keep Calling. No matter how many times you've called to white-

LEFT: If you do hunt from the ground you must think quickly and clearly and only draw at the optimum time.

Sometimes a natural blind is the best set up for a ground attack.

tails with little or no luck, try not to become discouraged. Be persistent and keep rattling and grunting. If you know mature bucks roam your area, that, along with confidence in your ability as a hunter, should be all the motivation you need. Just one magical experience — like rattling in a heavy-horned 8-point and killing him with a bow and arrow — is all it takes to change your outlook. Confidence is one of the deer hunter's most important intangibles. The more faith you have in yourself and any hunting tactic, the more mature

LEFT: It's easier to hide a hunter and cameraman on the ground than it is in a tree.

BELOW: Back cover is the key to any good ground set up.

RIGHT, ABOVE:
A cedar nest built
next to a major
cedar tree is one
of our favorite
ground set-ups.

RIGHT, BELOW:
Huge round bales
are perfect places
to set up.

bucks you'll tag.

Strangely enough, oversleeping that November morning was
a big step in our evolution as
deer hunters and callers. We
learned that we do not always
have to sit and wait for bucks to
appear. To the contrary, we realize we can sometimes take our
game to them.

One of our favorite rut-time tactics is to hone in on a small security cover where we think a mature buck might be holed up with a hot
doe. We stay mobile and do a lot of intense glassing. If we can spot one
or more bucks dogging a doe into a brushy ravine or sliver of timber,

that's obviously better yet.

That's when we make our move.

We make sure the wind is right, blowing from the cover to us, and sneak in for a ground assault. After setting up in a spot with good visibility and thick background cover, we rattle and grunt, and often we blow a snort-wheeze call. We try to sound like one or more intruder bucks. It drives some bucks mad! After a calling sequence, we pick up our bow, keep still and scan the cover intently. We've had some unbelievably fast and furious action, and we've shot some bruiser bucks that way.

After calling, we give it 20 to 30 minutes. If a buck is going to respond, it generally happens quickly. If we strike out, we might hit another small area or two with good access, such as a

LEFT: Once leaves fall trees become mighty open and it becomes increasingly difficult to hide at 20 feet off the ground.

Gun season more often finds us heading to a ground set up due to extended range.

brush-choked draw or strip of timber near a food plot or soybean field. But if the wind isn't right, or if we don't think we can slip into calling range undetected, we never risk it.

When in doubt, back out. Even when a bowshot looks and feels perfect and we think we've double-lunged a buck, neither Mark nor I get ahead of ourselves. If we don't see a buck go down, we might trail it a short distance. However, we invariably heed the old saying, "When in doubt, back out." You'll find that to be a recurring theme in this book.

It never hurts to wait four or five hours before trailing a buck, unless it rains, or coyotes frequent your hunting area. If you hit a deer too far back, we feel strongly that you ought to back out and wait 12 to 18 hours. You never want to jump a wounded buck, because he can go a long way on adrenaline alone. If his blood clots, you'll probably lose the trail.

When a buck's running trail (blood spraying out onto leaves or grass) slows to a walking trail (droplets of blood falling straight down to the ground) we stop and

Our good friend Michael Hanback with a huge 8-point he shot from a cedar ground blind in the middle of a CRP field.

back out immediately. That deer is not on a death run; rather, he's slowing down and probably looking for a place to lie down. We'll back out and give him time to do just that. More often than not, we'll come back and find him dead in his bed.

Most hunters are impatient when it comes to trailing bowshot deer. Think about this: You put so much time and effort into hunting a big deer and finally getting a shot at him. Why blow it by trailing him too fast? For more happy endings, go slow on a blood trail and back out when you need to. ∎

CHAPTER SEVEN

SACRED GROUND

Mark and I often dwell on the fun we had years ago during our "if it's brown, it's down" era. Man, we loved to shoot deer, and we made no apologies for it. But as we have gotten older and evolved as hunters, we're now into managing and hunting

mature bucks. We've gone crazy over planting food plots. We spend a lot of time, some (our wives) would say too much time, checking our crops and Biologic plots all summer. In fall, before we ever think of shooting a buck with a bow or gun, we study the animal's physique and try to determine how old he is — 2, 3, 4 or older? Do we have trail camera photos of the buck? Have we found its sheds? Have we ever seen the deer before? What will its rack score?

All creatures need a place to get away. Mature white-tailed bucks frequently use hidden sanctuaries. They're loners and reclusive by nature; they hate company, especially when gun season heats up. In November 2001, I slipped into one of our best sanctuaries and harvested my largest buck ever, a 163-inch, 10-point giant. Let's relive that memorable hunt, and discuss the methods Mark and I use to identify, create and hunt in and around what we call "sacred ground."

Ours has been quite a metamorphosis, and strangely it has come to this: In the early days we used any and every excuse to shoot every buck we saw; now we use any and every excuse not to shoot one. Mark and I often wonder if we've gone a little mad, and hindered our pleasure of the sport. However, we know there's no turning back — we're totally consumed. We eat, drink and sleep big bucks, and that's the way we like it.

To us, no two words carry more meaning than "sacred ground." The concept is simple: Through long-range observation and low-impact scouting, you hone in on a patch of dense ground cover where whitetails bed and escape pressure. Then, no matter the size of the sanctuary, you vow never to step foot inside it. When you do cheat and go in, you do so only a few times each season, and only when the wind and conditions are perfect. If you can show some restraint and live up to your vow, you should be able to harbor some mega bucks on your land.

Mark and I have had some phenomenal success doing just that in recent years. One incident in particular comes to mind.

It was mid-November and the eve of the Illinois shotgun opener. We desperately wanted to hunt a property that was home to one of our all-time favorite buck sanctuaries, but could we? We watched the Weather Channel all day. The wind was supposed to be perfect for slipping into the spot. Man, we were pumped, and we hardly slept a wink. Who sleeps the night before opening day anyway?

In the foggy, bone-chilling, predawn darkness, we crept onto the farm. The place is only 140 acres, but if food and cover are in place, it doesn't take much ground to hold a mature buck these days. We crept through the darkness and slipped silently to a tree-stand setup about 300 yards off the sacred ground. Steely light seeped into the woods, and I glassed toward the jungle of cover. Every time I see it, I dare say it's one of the best spots we've ever hunted. We elected to stay a safe distance as not to deposit any scent even close to the sanctuary.

Years ago, a farmer created a 15-acre field atop a long, broad ridge. I'm sure the old-timer who invested all that sweat equity had no idea he would have one day created some of the best wildlife habitat around. The field, now long abandoned, grew up with Osage orange, otherwise known as hedge apples in the Midwest, as well as honey locusts, multi-flora rose bushes and lots of cedars. Hardwoods on both sides of the cover cascaded down into valleys. A proverbial maze of fauna and flora was created over time!

What's more, that parcel is surrounded on three sides by Biologic plots and crop fields, which are usually planted in corn and/or soybeans. That feed plays a major role in driving deer to and from the sacred ground. If a mature buck feeds and noses does in one of the closest fields and then moves up to bed in the overgrown security cover, he might show up around 7 or 8 a.m. one morning, maybe even a little earlier. Big deer might bed in the thick stuff 100 to 200 yards from one of the other fields then rise to stretch and move around between 11 a.m. and 1 p.m. Or, a buck might get out of bed and skulk toward a staging area near yet another field or plot early or late in the afternoon. So it's an all-day spot. Once you sneak in there, you plan for a lengthy sit.

The pink sun glimmered on the horizon, the temperature dropped a few more degrees, and we shivered. Then BOOM! We flexed involuntarily as shotguns barked all around us, just as we knew they would. If you hunt a small property smartly and unobtrusively, the gun pressure on neighboring lands will actually improve your hunting. People stomping around and shooting on adjoining properties drive lots of deer to your sacred ground. Mark and I sat there the better part of the morning, wide-eyed, smiling and chattering like kids, glassing the veritable deer parade. At least 40 deer streamed into our scared ground, coming from all directions.

Most of them were does, which did not surprise us. We believe that when the intense pressure of gun season hits, mature bucks often hold their ground and don't sneak off for a safe haven until nightfall. For that reason, we've found that it's a good idea to allow a full night to pass before moving in on the second day to hunt your best stand. You have yet another advantage if your gun season hits during the November rut. If estrous does pile into cover on your side of the fence on Day 1, you can bet bucks will soon come looking for them.

Our opening-day observations made our plan for Day 2 a no-brainer. We knew the bedding area already held does, and more deer would likely pile in there overnight and the next day. If the wind held steady we would take a chance, move in and hunt our best "brushy ridge stand," which was located just inside the sacred ground at a pinch point where the ridgetop of thick cover is the narrowest and the hardwood timber is the closest.

Things were running smooth as clockwork until…

My cell phone blared early the next morning. "Go on without me," Mark growled. I could tell by the tone of his voice that he was not a happy camper, and then I found out why. He had a flat tire. "You've got a long walk, and I don't want to hold you up. That spot is too hot. Go kill a big deer." He hung up. I swear I saw smoke coming out my phone.

As luck would have it, Jim Howell, one of our other cameramen and friends, just happened to be staying at my camp. I rousted Jim out of bed and hollered, "Get your stuff, and let's go!"

The brushy ridge stand is located about 500 yards from where we park our truck. We get there early and walk slow and easy. We never use a flashlight in the morning. We creep along as silently as possible, taking great pains not to jump any bedded deer. We carry our jackets, wear light clothes and try not to sweat. That would be a chore this morning, as it was humid and foggy, "close" as we hunters like to say.

Jim and I snuck along, dropping down into ditches and ravines and scrambling up banks and ridges. We crossed a creek and paused momentarily to rinse our boots. We've found that after doing that, deer rarely pick up our scent trail on the other side of a stream. We pressed on, going up and down, trying to avoid touching the thick brush all the while. Lugging his camera gear, Jim began perspiring profusely. I felt for my partner, and I knew that if it cleared off and the temperature cooled down at sunrise, he would be in for a long, chilly sit. But there was nothing I could do about it. I was trying my best to take it easy. Besides, I had a bad case of big deer on my mind.

I urged Jim on and he hung tough, as usual.

Finally, we climbed brushy ridge … and all hell broke loose. A flock of turkeys flushed from their roosts, cackling and putting, their wings thumping against trees and making all sorts of noise. I cringed and froze. Thankfully, no deer blew or crashed off. We crept the final yards, climbed quietly to our stands and pulled up our gear.

Dawn cracked, the fog lifted and the air cleared and cooled a few degrees. Jim would have no time to shiver this morning. The deer parade had already begun. And this time they were bucks!

I don't recall exactly how many bucks streamed past our stand that morning – six, eight, maybe 10. I do remember one gorgeous, 2-year-old buck. And I certainly remember passing on a borderline shooter, a gray, thick-bodied 10-point.

Then, around eight o'clock, he showed up and dwarfed them all.

"Big shooter, big shooter, oh man, he's a giant," I whispered to Jim. The big 10 tipped through the brush and cedars, his rack way out past his ears, tall tines glistening in the sun. He was without a doubt the biggest deer I had seen all season and probably one of the largest bucks in that area.

It was like you flicked a switch in the tree, only moments before Jim and I had been settling in, readying our gear and admiring the parade of bucks. Now things were chaotic, spinning out of control. It can get that way when two guys are trying to

act as one and film and shoot a huge buck, their minds reeling and their hearts tripping like jackhammers.

I pushed the panic button and quizzed Jim, "Are you on him, are you on him, are you on him?"

Jim hissed frantically back, "No, no, no I'm not."

When you're filming a deer hunt, the shooter's view is usually much different from the cameraman's. I stared at the bruiser at 40 yards through my gun scope, and I could have killed him at any time. But a big cedar tree blocked Jim's look at the deer. Eventually the old boy vanished, trailing a doe into the thick, dense cover of "brushy ridge."

We sat there in awkward silence for a while. What was there to say? We wanted to kill the deer, but only on video, and we just didn't get the job done. That's one of the perils of filming, and you must have the

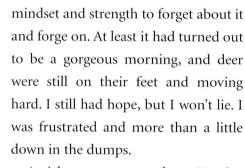

mindset and strength to forget about it and forge on. At least it had turned out to be a gorgeous morning, and deer were still on their feet and moving hard. I still had hope, but I won't lie. I was frustrated and more than a little down in the dumps.

A picker-upper came about 20 minutes later when I spotted yet another heavy-bodied buck. I looked closer…it was him, the big 10-point! My goodness, he had popped back out! You couldn't miss those dagger-like tines. I aimed my shotgun and whispered to Jim, "Are you on him?"

I'll never forget his wonderful reply, "Yes, I am."

I squeezed the trigger and the buck collapsed.

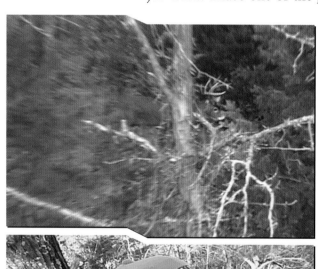

Our excitement was contagious. While trying to calm our nerves, Jim and I high-fived, talked and laughed awhile. It was as if someone had just lifted a gorilla off our backs. Strangely, killing the buck on video the second time around made the hunt all that sweeter.

The buck was about 100 yards away, and his white belly was shining in the sunlight. We knew he was down. Then the post-production work began in our stands. We filmed cutaways and informational tidbits, doing all the little things that create a solid, entertaining video. It sometimes puts a little damper on the celebration, especially when you know you have a gargantuan buck on the ground. But we never take our work lightly. We pride ourselves in doing all the little things, and doing them right.

As we worked, deer kept streaming by and piling into the brushy cover. Several does trotted past our tree, and I stopped during one segment to glass a mature 8-point as he sneaked along a ridge. I finally looked at Jim and said, "Man, this is a morning from heaven! We could sit up here and watch deer all day. But I've just got to get down and go see our buck!"

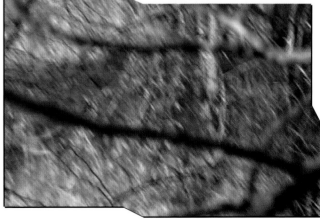

I scrambled down the tree, hustled over there and put my hands on the best deer I had shot to date. Turning the huge antlers in my hands, I looked straight into the camera and said, "This is a hunt I'll always remember, and one I'll always cherish. It's one of my happiest days." I meant every word.

The only downside to hunting brushy ridge is getting a heavyweight buck out of there. The drag out is long and tough, literally a pain in the rear. Jim and I worked our butts off. My partner really had the sweat droplets pouring now. But the glow on his face told me he didn't mind it one darn bit. He had done his job and a good one at that. I was extremely grateful for his help.

When we got back to my truck, I called Mark's cell and said gloomily, "We shot a small one, you'd better come and take a look at it." Mark had fixed his flat and was in a little better spirits.

Brother made it over to my camp in record time. He hopped out of his truck, took one look at the awesome 10-point, gave each of us a bear hug and roared, "You dogs, way to go!" I know my brother, and I could tell he was a little blue about missing out on the hunt. But he was happy for me and elated for Jim,

who hung tough not once but twice, and pulled off some great cinematography that unforgettable day on sacred ground.

BILL MARCHEL

LESSONS
LEARNED

Identifying Sacred Ground. When we talk about sacred ground, we're referring to a major bedding/security area for whitetails. It might be an overgrown crop field or clear-cut – or a pine thicket or a cedar glade – or a nasty, brushy draw or bottom. You get the picture. A lot of deer bed in the thick cover throughout the year. A lot more pile into the jungle when the gun pressure heats up on nearby properties.

When creating a sacred ground, consider the property's total acreage. If you've got 1,000 acres and 500 acres are good, thick

cover, you might set aside half or a third of it as sacred ground. If you hunt an 80- to 100-acre parcel, a third of which is cover and the rest open ground, obviously the entire third ought to be your sacred ground. Just use a common-sense approach as to how much security cover is available on a property.

To coincide with cover, you need feed. If there isn't a good food source within a reasonable distance of your sacred ground, or if the food isn't sufficient enough to sustain or maintain a deer herd, you won't hold many deer – no matter how thick and secluded it

∾

is. Always be conscious of the amount of food that's available in the area, and the distance from the food to the security cover. If the food isn't there, deer are not going to stay.

The size of a sanctuary doesn't matter. We've got one piece of ground that's only 50 acres. It is surrounded on all four sides by another landowner. The parcel consists of 20 acres of cover, 20 acres of crops and 10 acres of CRP ground. We never walk into the 20 acres of cover. We leave it as a sacred ground, and that brushy refuge fills up with deer when the guns start booming.

We put a huge emphasis on the hunting pressure on neighboring properties, and try to designate a sacred ground as far away from that pressure as possible. That way, deer feel comfortable coming to the secluded cover from all directions, especially once the season starts. Deer will stay there all season if they feel safe. If

We are very fanatical about penetration within certain areas. Hunting sheds in March is one of the few times we'll even visit some spots.

you leave your sacred ground alone — if you don't hassle and jump deer or shoot too close to their sanctuary —deer will find the cover and keep coming back.

Don't worry about mature bucks finding your sacred ground. They're masters at finding sanctuaries. They know where the pressure is, and where it isn't. We believe deer learn about a major bedding area and pass that knowledge on to their yearlings. Those deer pass it down the line, and so on. The longer you keep and protect a sacred ground, the better it becomes over time.

When possible we'll use lakes or waterways to lead us to sacred ground edges.

ABOVE: Thick cedar glades are unbelievably good cover for deer. We seldom walk through these types of areas.

RIGHT: A huge rub in or around thick cover is a sure sign a nice buck lives close by.

Think about it. Why can you drive through a state park and see hundreds of deer at midday? When you motor just outside the park, you can't see a doe or a buck to save your life. Whitetails know the location of sacred ground, so set aside your own park. Deer will find it and use it.

One last point: We sometimes must adjust a sacred ground from year to year. We might hunt a spot and realize we're bumping too

We're careful not to interrupt certain areas when we hunt. If we choose to take a doe, we do it in places far away from tight sanctuaries.

many deer on the way to or from a stand. If you constantly bump deer, chances are you are walking through a bedding area. Well, stay out of there! However, bumping deer does have its benefits, because it is one of the best ways to find and identify sacred ground, especially when you're hunting a new property.

Creating and Enhancing Sacred Ground. Say you're hunting 80 acres and there's no dad-gum cover on the place. Well, you can create a sanctuary. Plant 30 or 40 acres of switch grass. Deer love that stuff. It's one of the thickest, most natural places for deer to bed. Or, plant 30 acres of pines. They provide especially good thermal cover. Also consider small clear-cuts. The secondary growth will provide cover and much-needed nutrition.

If you already have some thick cover, enhance it. Do some timber-stand improvement to create second growth, or thicken a sanctuary by planting some evergreens or switch grass. Mature bucks are always attracted to thick cover.

Again, you can have the best securi-

ty cover for miles, but if there's no quality feed nearby, deer will not stay long. Reverse that trend by planting food plots in strategic places. Plant plots tight to a sanctuary. That creates travel corridors and funnels from the bedding area to the feed. Above all, stay out of the sacred ground. We hang tree stands on the plot edges and along travel corridors leading toward security cover, and we only hunt them when the wind is perfect. It's one of the ways we hunt mature bucks without pressuring them.

For small plots near security cover, we

LEFT: Field roads are perfect travel routes to and from stands.

BELOW: Locked, loaded and ready. Only diligent practice will have you ready when the moment of truth arrives.

plant Biologic, clover and/or soy-beans. These plants create feed and diverse edges, and they allow us to see more deer from our fringe stands. If we put in a huge plot, we like to create even more security cover and extend the bedding area out into the feed. In those cases, we typically plant corn, which grows tall and provides great cover.

By creating more than one food plot on a property, you can decipher deer travel routes. It also gives you an advantage; you gain options for hunting different stands on different winds, depending on where your plots are located in relation to your sacred ground.

Suppose you plant a small Biologic plot — let's call it a secondary food

ABOVE: Hunting the edge of thick cover allows for good access and easier wind direction availability. Deer use the edges of cover for a lot of their travel routes.

RIGHT: A brushy draw jetting into 10-year growth CRP. Fantastic cover for huge whitetail bucks.

source —at one end of an 80-acre parcel. Then you put in a main

food source — maybe two to five acres of corn or beans — at the other end. Suddenly, you've created a situation that puts deer on their feet and gives them a reason to travel from one end of the property to the other. If your sacred ground is somewhere in

the middle, then you've got options for hanging multiple stands and hunting them on different winds.

Stay Out! One of the most common statements we hear from hunters is that human pressure doesn't really bother mature bucks. Mark and I snicker every time we hear that. It's as far from the truth as you can possibly get. Pressure bothers old bucks more than you know.

Hunters are nosy. They want to explore every inch of a property. They roam around and look for rubs, scrapes and other deer sign. Mark and I are just the opposite. We

hunt unobtrusively and leave deer alone as much as possible. A mature buck needs a sanctuary, just like you need a space, a little bedroom where nobody bothers you, and where you can get away from people and pressure. A buck needs his space, too, so give it to him.

We seldom go into a

ABOVE: We'll use cornfields as cover to go into and or around certain sanctuaries. Standing corn provides great cover for open food plots.

LEFT: Our good friend Joe Shults with an awesome buck taken on the fringe of a 100-acre sanctuary on his farm.

buck's bedroom, except to recover a deer we've shot. We might go in there and hunt sheds in March, but that's about it. However, we do often hunt the fringes of our sacred grounds.

Even when hunting the fringes, access is the key to success. For starters, the wind must be right, blowing from a bedding area to you. We often use the edges of creeks and lakes, or field roads or old timber trails, to sneak toward cover. We also use standing corn for cover.

We especially like to hunt the edges of a sanctuary where acorns are falling, or where food plots are planted just to the north, south, east or west. Deer use those edges heavily when moving from bed to feed. Bucks walk the edges, checking for does going in and out of the bedding area. That's where you need to set up, but only when the wind is right.

Keep this in mind. If you see an old buck moving to or from a bedding area —especially if he's going toward it — nine times out of 10, he will circle downwind of the cover and sniff for does and danger before he steps inside the bedroom.

Mark and I are low-impact hunters, but we admit we cheat every once in a while.

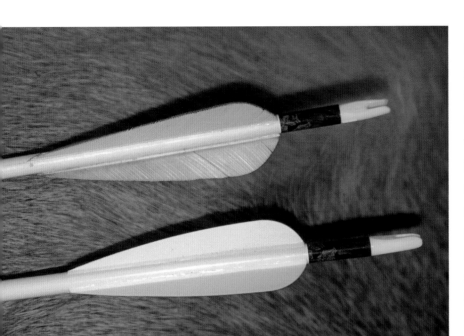

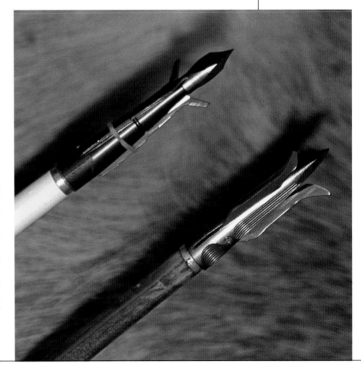

Once in a blue moon we'll penetrate a buck's bedroom, but only when we get the perfect wind and only when the conditions are right. Those conditions are: a) the rut has deer moving hard throughout the day; b) gun season has pushed a lot of deer into a sacred ground; or c) it is late season and deer are holed up in thick, thermal cover.

Let me emphasize, it's not like we sneak into a bedding area every day. Far from it! Throughout the course of a hunting season, we might hunt inside a sanctuary two or three times and only when the wind and conditions are perfect.

Earlier in this chapter, I mentioned how we like one full night to pass before hunting tight to or inside a sanctuary on a small piece of ground (maybe 50 to 150 acres). I'd like to expand on that. We hunt larger properties where it where it sometimes takes two, three or four days of gun pressure on the outside before big bucks hit our sacred grounds. We've got one farm of about 1,000 acres, and it generally takes three or four days for it to fill up with deer from the pressure across the fences. It all depends on the size of your hunting spot and how many deer you have. Still, once the guns start booming, bucks will enter your safe haven. It might take one to four days for them to get there, but they will show up. Keep watching.

Finally, we manage intensively and, therefore, shoot a lot of does. However, we avoid killing does near a sacred ground. We don't want shotguns or muzzleloaders booming near a bedding area. We never like to blood trail deer into good cover, or drag 'em out. We certainly never field dress a deer in a sacred ground. Again, staying out is the key.

Is Sacred Ground For Everyone? Our sacred ground principle sounds simple enough. But can it always be done in today's hunting arena? Probably not, as we have learned over the years. You certainly can't control the comings and goings of other hunters on a public area or even on a lease you share with other people. Even if you own or lease exclusive hunting rights to a farm, you might be successful raising and harboring big bucks for a few years, but people will eventually find out about it. Neighboring hunters will exert more pressure on the perimeters of your sanctuaries and bedding areas. Sadly, poachers might slip into them. You really need to patrol and keep a close eye on all your lands.

If you're managing deer, here's one thing you can do. We try to convince adjoining landowners to commit to a management program similar to ours. Everybody plants food plots and sets aside sanctuaries. Everybody agrees, without faltering, to let young bucks walk, and they harvest plenty of does. Creating a consortium of landowners with similar goals is difficult, but if you can pull it off, great. Everyone will enjoy better hunting for years to come. As your neighbors see and shoot more mature bucks, it decreases the pressure on your land. That will help you manage and harbor more big deer. ∎

CHAPTER EIGHT

LAST CALL

Back in the fall of 1995, the full moon in November, which Native Americans called the hunter's moon and which some people now refer to as the rutting moon, came extremely late. As I recall it didn't wax full until the 17th of the month, and I believe that was a big reason the Midwestern rut was a week or so later than normal that year. Anyhow, since the deer movement was slow in the part of Iowa where our good friend Steve Stoltz and I were hunting, we bounced around from farm to farm, and from ridge to bottom within those farms, scouting, observing and trying to find a hot spot where a good buck might be dogging a hot doe or two.

Happily, we found some smoking rubs, scrapes and big tracks in "Booner Hollow." We just love to hunt that place when the wind and rut conditions are right. As its name implies, we spot more muscle-bound, huge-racked bucks there than anyplace else we hunted at the time.

Stoltz, who was helping us out and running the camera, and I slipped into the area early on the morning of November 20$^{th.}$ A zillion stars blinked in the ebony sky and a cool, gentle wind blew out of the northwest—perfect, since we were coming in from the south, and since past observations had showed that most of the deer movement in and around Booner Hollow came from the north. We

■ Over the past decade, calling has been our best tactic for coaxing whitetails within bow range. On many of our video hunts, the last call that mature bucks heard came from our rattling horns or grunt call. Here we'll share the hair-raising tale of a 20-inch-wide 8-point that charged into my rattles one November morning. Terry and I will then follow up with a no-holds-barred collection of our thoughts on when, where and how to call deer.

sneaked quietly along the edge of a pasture field on a ridge and climbed into our stands just back in a finger of brushy timber. It was a good thing we got there and settled in an hour before daybreak. When the pink sun rose and glimmered, we spotted deer bedded in the next finger of woods across the ridge field, and across the big, long draw we call Booner Hollow.

Deer movement was slow in the soft, pastel light of dawn. The lighter it got, the more the temperature dropped. We shivered and waited. An hour later, with the sun glistening white-hot in the hollow, things began to heat up. I swept my binoculars up and down the brushy draw and started seeing pieces of deer—legs, flickering ears, patches of brown and white hide and the occasional tine. I wasn't

sure how many deer or what mix of animals was in there, but I thought and hoped at least one of them was a huge old buck tending a hot little doe.

I waited and watched for 45 minutes or so, hoping the deer would eventually pop out of the hollow and move toward us on a pattern of natural movement. Finally, I figured that was not going to happen, so I reached for the rattling horns hanging on a limb near my stand.

"It's about time, hey, hey, hey," Stoltz whispered, giving his trademark little laugh. "I would've rattled 30 minutes ago."

"Well, you aren't doing the rattling or the hunting," I hissed back through clenched teeth. It's always a sparring match with Stoltz and me, in a friendly and competitive sort of way.

I cracked the horns for about 20 seconds. Nothing major, just a good, solid rattling volley. I had just hung up the antlers and picked up my bow when Stoltz flicked on his camera and whispered, "Deer coming!"

A young buck with a twig-like rack sprinted straight to the base of our tree and stood there, gawking round and round. I smiled and wondered, "And just what in the world would you do if you saw two big bruisers fighting over here? You'd get your little butt…"

Suddenly I caught the flash of another deer. I cut my saucer-wide eyes down and left and spotted a hog charging in, the hair bristling

on his neck, his wide and heavy rack glistening in the mid-morning sun. The little buck shot away like somebody lit his hide on fire. The big boy rolled in to 30 yards and I drew my bow—just as a third buck charged onto the scene! The old deer took one look at this immature 8-point, raised his hackles higher, snorted and charged off after the intruder.

The agility and speed of whitetails never ceases to amaze me. Before I could let down my draw, all three bucks had crashed back into the brushy draw where, it was obvious to me now, at least one hot doe was hanging out.

"Hey, hey, hey, pretty cool, huh?" laughed Stoltz. "Try to call 'em up again."

I waited 10 minutes for things to settle down, and just to get Stoltz's goat a bit, I suppose. Then I reached for the horns. I must tell you my confidence was not exactly soaring. It's hard enough to call a mature buck into bow range once, but twice? Figuring I had nothing to lose, I whacked the horns for another 15 or 20 seconds.

After a calling sequence, whether I brim with confidence or not, I always go through the same little ritual. I remain standing in my stand, hang up the horns, pick up my bow, clip on my release, scan the woods, *stay focused.* On this day, it paid off big time.

The 140-inch buck sounded like an elephant crashing back out of the draw. He charged toward us again, grunting like a market hog, muscles rippling and the hair bristling on his back and neck. I caught a flash behind him and shivered for a nanosecond. This was, after all, Booner Hollow, and who knew what might be coming next. But it was just the two little bucks the old boy had run off earlier, and now they knew their place, bringing up the rear.

I immediately turned my attention back to the big deer

and whispered, "Oh no!" He circled steadily downwind, like most bucks do when coming to the ruckus of a fight. The buck trotted straight through the thick cover and then straight through our wind and scent stream. I turned in my stand, followed him and cringed, figuring he would smell a rat any minute. But he kept trotting closer and closer! It's easy to forget or neglect the details, like showering and using an odor-neutralizer, but it's critical. Both Stoltz and I were sparkling clean and as scent-free as possible that morning, and I think it helped us.

The buck's built-in GPS system allowed him to home in on the sound of my horns. When he stopped charging, he was precisely 12 steps from my stand. Amazing! My arrow sliced through the air and the buck wheeled and crashed away. His little buddies followed him a ways, then veered back into the brushy hollow where at least one hot doe was still waiting.

"Now that was really cool," Stoltz giggled as we high-fived in the tree.

When in doubt, back out. You've read that phrase several times in this book, and that is exactly what

we did once again. I felt pretty good about the shot—it might have been just a tad back—but we didn't see or hear the 8-point crash down. After tracking a ways and not liking what we saw, we pulled off the blood trail. Again, it is a tough thing to do, but the right thing to do. This time we waited almost a full day before resuming the track.

The next morning was a carbon copy of the previous day, sunny and crisp, when the woods are vibrant and full of life, when the sights, sounds and smells of nature are truly wonderful. Upon cresting a little hogback, I looked down through the shining woods and yelled, "Look at that!" I ran up to the buck, knelt, and twisted his 20-inch-wide rack in my hands. I gawked at his long brow tines, looked at Stoltz and said, "I've always wanted to kill a really wide-racked buck. He's got that. I've always wanted to shoot a really heavy-racked buck. He's got that, too. And look at his body, it's gigantic! It's hard to imagine an awesome buck like this coming to rattling not once, but twice!"

Stoltz didn't say anything, which was unusual, but he didn't have to. The look on his face said, "Now how cool is that!"

CHARLES J. ALSHEIMER

LESSONS LEARNED

When to Call Whitetails. We have found that the prime window for calling whitetails here in the Midwest is open from October 25 to November 25. Within that window, October 30 to November 10 is typically the best. That is when big deer are drunk on testosterone and up and moving, wandering through the woods with their noses glued to the ground. We call them "cruisers." Cruising around in search of the first estrous does, the bucks are primed to come to your rattles, grunts, bleats or grunt-snort-wheezes.

Pre-October 25, the only time we'll call is if we see a mature buck walking though the woods, apparently not coming toward our tree stand. We'll give him some light contact grunts in hopes of turning him our way. Sometimes it works, but most of the time it doesn't.

Once the rut is over and the calling window slams shut, we keep rattling and grunting a little bit into early December, hoping to attract a buck looking for one last hot doe. But later in the month, since deer are wired and stressed and locked in on food, we call very little if at all.

ABOVE: We like to use the Lohman Dynamite Rattler for close in coaxing. The small device is amazingly realistic, allowing for great sound with minimal movement.

LEFT: Choosing the correct pair of antlers can lead to success. We prefer an 8- or 10-point set from 100 to 130 inches. Fresh sheds with a high ring seem to produce very good results.

Grunting can be effective anytime of day, but Terry and I have found that rattling almost always works best in the mornings. A chilly, calm, high-pressure November morning is great. We like to set up downwind of a bedding area or a terrain funnel that leads to a thick sacred ground. That is where bucks cruise. They can hear the ring of our horns a long way, and they just might respond.

Weather-wise, the first cold front in mid-October or the first major snowfall in November will get deer on their feet and moving, making them highly susceptible to your calls.

Where to call. Rattling and grunting work anywhere in the country, but there is no doubt that farms and ranches with sound deer-management practices and low hunting pressure yield the best results. Since we started seriously managing our farms a few years ago—putting in food plots, harvesting lots of does and tightly controlling the hunting pressure on all our properties—the number of mature bucks coming to our calls has increased dramatically.

Our specific calling locations have evolved over the years. We've begun to set up less on deer sign and more on visible structure. For example, instead of always looking for areas with big rubs or scrapes, we often simply hang our tree stands on hogback ridges, along field edges or in open fencerows where

we can see and glass lots of country. We've had so much luck with calling late in October and into mid-November that we now simply set up where we can see a cruiser buck a long way off, and then try to pull him close with rattles, loud grunts or other calls.

While Terry and I like to call where the terrain is open or semi-open, we always try to put some type of barrier *behind* our stands. An impenetrable windrow, a deep river, a steep bluff and a fenced field are good examples of some barriers we look for. When a mature deer hears your calls, he likes to move and circle downwind, trying to smell the fighting, grunting or bleating "deer." But if you

Mossy Oak's Darrell Daigre with a 150" 8 pt. that died coming to a short rattling sequence. Terry lays the scene down for our videos.

can block a buck with a terrain barrier, you force him to come in from the side or out front where he can't wind you and bust you.

Speaking of the wind, I'd like to make a major point. If you spot a good buck moving anywhere on the downwind side of your stand, don't call to him. Almost inevitably he'll take a few more steps, get dead downwind, stick his nose in the air and bust you. Alert a mature buck to the presence of a human in his core area just once, and that will make him doubly tough to hunt and call on subsequent days.

Anytime natural deer movement is slow in early to mid-November, Terry and I sometimes bag our tree stands and go on a ground attack. This is when calling and mobility go hand in hand. We put the wind in our face and sneak from one thick, accessible bedding area to the next, trying to find that magical spot where a mature deer is holed up with a hot doe. We always set up where the wind blows from the cover to us, and then rattle, grunt and often toss in a few grunt-snort-wheezes. We've had some incredible action and killed some great bucks that way, like the heavy-horned 8-point that Terry rattled up in Chapter 6.

Whether you're hunting on the ground or 20 feet up a tree, try to put a patch of thick cover and the sun somewhere at your back. That way, a buck can't hear your rattles or grunts, look through the open woods and see no deer over there. You trick him into thinking that deer are fighting or breeding in thick cover behind your stand, so there's a decent chance he'll move closer to investigate.

Your visibility is best when the sun rises or sets behind you. It is easy to pick up an incoming buck when sunlight glints on his hide or rack. Also, when a deer walks to your rattles or grunts into the sun, it is almost impossible for him to pick you off if you set up well in cover and don't move around too much.

How to call. My hunt for the big 8-point illustrates a key point: Whether you're rattling, grunting or bleating, most of the time it's best to do it sparingly. I just hit the horns a few times that November day, rattling for

Gun season in many states hits during the prime calling window. In our opinion that window is 10/25 - 11/25 in the Midwest, specifically 10/30 - 11/10.

only 15 to 20 seconds, and the 140-incher popped back out the draw, ran within 12 steps of my tree and gave me a good shot. When the rut is right, sometimes just a few clicks or grunts are all you need. Deer are curious and inquisitive creatures. The smart hunter calls sparingly and toys with that curiosity.

Terry and I never enter the woods without a M.A.D grunt tube dangling around our necks. Early, late or during the rut, in the morning or in the afternoon, we'll grunt at a big deer we see cruis-

One slight call on a grunt call can be all it takes to lure a giant out of thick cover and into your sights. Deer are curious creatures, smart hunters toy with that curiosity.

ing through the woods. What have you got to lose? A curious or rutting buck might turn toward your stand and walk right in.

We have the most success grunting to deer we see cruising 20 to maybe 60 yards out of bow range. In this situation, instead of just calling aimlessly, we watch a buck and work him. A mature deer's body language will tell you when and how much to call. If you grunt and a buck pins back his ears, raises the hair on his back and pops his tail erect, call again when you're sure he can't look up and bust you. That deer is rutted up and ready! A couple of aggressive grunts might be all it takes to reel him right to your tree. On the other hand, if a deer's demeanor is more laid back, you probably ought to grunt softly and sparingly at him.

Calling and mobility go together. We'll often move from bedding area to bedding area and call with the wind in our face.

Choosing the correct rattling horns is important. We prefer an 8- or 10-point, 100- to 130-inch pair of antlers. For close-in coaxing, we like the Lohman Dynamite Rattler. The small device makes an amazingly realistic sound of two bucks fighting, and it is easy to carry and use with minimal movement.

Early in the pre-rut when whitetails are locked into bed-to-feed patterns, Terry and I call sparingly early in the morning and late in the afternoon, when most deer move on a natural pattern. But when the short but sweet cruising phase hits and rolls right into the rut, we sometimes rattle and grunt all day long. You never

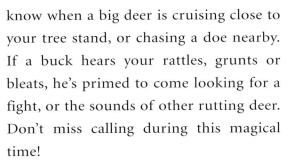

RIGHT: We'll often give a soft bleat or grunt to stop a deer just prior to releasing an arrow.

BELOW: Anytime or anywhere we hunt you can bet that a grunt call will be hanging from our necks.

know when a big deer is cruising close to your tree stand, or chasing a doe nearby. If a buck hears your rattles, grunts or bleats, he's primed to come looking for a fight, or the sounds of other rutting deer. Don't miss calling during this magical time!

One thing you ought to do is mix your calls, especially during the rut. It's only natural, and you never know which sound might appeal to a buck. For example, intersperse a series of tending grunts with a few estrous doe bleats to create the illusion of a buck dogging a doe. A nearby buck might come to the grunts, the bleats or the combination of calls. It doesn't matter which sound he likes, so long as he charges in!

Spicing up our rattling sequences with grunt-snort-wheezes is something we've been doing a lot in recent years. In our opinion, the call mimics a mature buck's warning signal to another buck just before a fight breaks out, or just after a battle is over. The M.A.D. Grunt-Snort-Wheeze is one of the best calls we've tried on mature bucks tending or chasing does. It gives you another vocalization to try in hopes of pulling in a rutting buck. It should be noted that the grunt-snort-wheeze is perhaps the *worse* call you can cast a subordinate deer's way. A 1$^1/_2$- or 2$^1/_2$-year-old buck that hears a warning wheeze is apt to turn tail and run for the hills if there is a dominant buck patrolling the territory!

Here's one last point, and it's major. The minute you finish a rattling or grunting sequence, go immediately into stealth mode. Hang up your horns or call, grab your bow or gun, keep still and scan the woods in case a buck shows up fast, coming either on the run or sneaking in. Many

LEFT: It's a great idea to replay the shot and the deer's exit from your stand. High excitement can cloud one's judgment once on the ground tracking.

BELOW: The first snowfall of each year can yield awesome calling results, especially if the flakes fly during November.

people fumble around with their horns or calls, sit down in their stands, fidget around too much and spook deer that were coming to their calls!

So chill out and watch for a buck to work close. When you spot one doing that, don't get too excited and overdo it. Just grunt or click the horns enough to get and keep a buck's attention. Do it when a deer turns his head away, takes a step or is hidden by a tree or brush. If you grunt or rattle too much in a buck's face, he'll see you move. Or he won't see any deer over there, which might make him nervous enough to turn and leave.

The last sound many deer hear come from our rattling devices and grunt calls.

On one of those glorious days when you coax a big deer all the way into bow range, wait for him to turn broadside or quarter away. Then draw and grunt or bleat with your voice. The second the deer stops, let fly, follow through and watch the arrow disappear into his side. In whitetail hunting, it doesn't get much better than that. ■

POSTSCRIPT

This is a true story, I promise. Earlier in the morning before we fetched my buck from Booner Hollow, Stoltz and I went to a nearby spot. He hunted while I filmed. An hour after sunrise, another 140-incher, this one a 9-point, charged in to Stoltz's rattles and grunts, and my friend killed him. Two mature bucks rattled up and shot with bows in one day, on video no less! It was totally cool, and it proves a point. During the rut, when the calling window is flung wide open and the mature bucks are coming to the horns, by all means keep rattling!

LEFT: Calling can work anywhere but farms with sound management tactics and low pressure seem to yield our best responses.

BELOW: Mark Drury and Steve Stoltz with a pair of 140's shot 24 hours apart both coming to a call.

CHAPTER NINE

SLAVES TO THEIR STOMACHS

Back in December 1999, I flew solo for a few days at our Iowa farm, just sitting and watching hungry whitetails pouring onto our food plots. Terry and I weren't filming that much late in the season back then, and I was enjoying the downtime and the rest, because we had been hard at it for weeks, bowhunting and filming every day in several states during the wild and crazy November rut.

It was cold but nothing drastic, quite pleasant actually for doing things I truly love – observing deer, studying their movements and behavioral quirks and trying to get into their heads. Each evening I'd see this nice 8-point, which I guessed to be 3$\frac{1}{2}$ years old, slip into the back end of a soybean field. He was no monster, but he dwarfed the other

■ Dr. Grant Woods is one of the top wildlife biologists in North America. He once told us, "Deer are slaves to their own stomachs." We took that to heart, and over the past few years, we've discovered many things about the critical relationship between whitetails and food sources. At no time was that relationship more evident than during a snowy, brutally cold, 10-day stretch one mid-December. We battled the elements and hunted one of our best late-season fields, and I shot a phenomenal 220-pound, 9-point buck. Here's a look at everything Terry and I have learned about food sources and nutrition, and the importance they hold for successfully managing and hunting whitetails.

1$\frac{1}{2}$ - and 2$\frac{1}{2}$ -year-old bucks he was running with. One day I moved in for a closer look.

I climbed into a box blind we had built on the field, and set my shotgun in the corner. I had a buck tag left, and even though we weren't rolling tape, carrying my gun just seemed like the sensible thing to do. An hour before dark deer streamed toward the beans— does, immature bucks and then the 8-point I had gotten to know so well over the last few days. He walked toward my stand and then underneath it! I glassed his muscular body and studied his 135-class rack. I reached for my gun, started to raise it, then set it back down.

As darkness neared, the buck fed awhile and walked away, his rack looking 10 inches larger than it really was. The mind games began when he disappeared. Had I done the right thing? What was I thinking? Would I ever see the deer again? That was the first 3 1/2-year-old buck I had ever passed in my life. Little did I know it would turn out to be a benchmark in my hunting career.

Terry and I can't be everywhere at once, so we didn't hunt that farm at all the next fall during the rut. But we were back there the next gun season, and this time the weather was brutally perfect. It was dangerously cold, and the northwest wind whipped 20 to 30 mph, sending the wind chill plummeting to minus 40. We were all fired up, knowing the hungry, rut-thin deer would move hard and early onto our feed fields in the evenings, and they would linger there in the mornings.

In fact, we had focussed on late-season hunting more and more in recent years. We see more mature bucks on their feet in December than we do in October and November. There's a simple reason for that: Big deer in the post-rut cannot resist the delectable smorgasbord of high-quality food.

One afternoon, Terry, our friend Mike Joggerst and I trudged toward the familiar box blind on the edge of the beans, crouching and leaning into the wind, battling the nearly whiteout conditions. The swirling snow stung our faces like bees, and the arctic air blasted deep into our lungs. We felt some relief after climbing into the wind-blocking blind. Still, we shivered and moved like icemen.

"Terry, I can't remember ever hunting in such extreme cold," I

whispered, trying to position my nearly frozen camera.

Joggerst nodded, but Terry didn't. His ears were crimson, mildly frostbitten on the tips, and I think he worried they would shatter and fall off if he moved.

We sat out of the wind for an hour and started feeling better. An hour before dark, our blood started boiling. Nearly 20 does and young bucks appeared first. The deer stepped out of the timber, jogged through the snow for the tallest beans and plunged their heads into them. They were spooky in the wind, like they always are, but they were so hungry they hardly came up for air.

"There!" Terry hissed, his frozen voice cracking.

I cut my eyes to the buck and let out my trademark gasp, "Ooohh." I'd know that buck anywhere. It was the same one I had passed last gun season, and he was now a tremendous, tall-racked 9-point! He had grown 20 inches of bone on his head since I had last seen him, including a G-4 on his left antler. I cracked an icy smile. The buck had survived, stayed home on our farm and even walked the same trail into the beans that he had used the previous year. I got this warm, fuzzy feeling all over.

Then I morphed back into predatory mode. There would be no passing the buck now. We would kill the fully mature beast if we got the chance.

The buck hopped a fence on the edge of the woods about 200 yards

away. He worked his way closer, feeding like a harvesting machine and bullying his way through the does and young bucks. Terry eased his shotgun barrel out the port hole, locked in and then hissed, "Oh no!"

A flock of turkeys that had been feeding alongside the deer suddenly got the wind jitters and exploded into the air, cackling, putting and flying off to roost. That started a melee. Deer scrambled for the timber, leaping and bounding through the snow, their white flags waving bye-bye. The whole field cleared, and our hearts chilled. We sat and waited in our igloo, hoping the power of the soybeans would be too much, and that the big deer would return at dusk.

He didn't.

Back at camp that night, we thawed out and flew into another one of our strategy sessions. This one was short and to the point.

"Mark, that is the oldest, biggest, most gorgeous buck on the farm, and the northwest wind is perfect for where he's coming out into the beans," Terry said as he gently massaged his burning, blood-red ears. "Let's set our sights on him the rest of the season."

How could I argue with that?

We battled the extreme condi-

tions for days, hunting for the big deer both mornings and evenings. The beans drew hundreds of deer like magnets, including some pretty bucks in the 130- and 140-class. But we never laid eyes on the giant again.

Life has this annoying way of interrupting your deer hunting. I had to leave for a business meeting, but Terry kept hunting. He didn't lay eyes on the big buck. The next weekend, the last of the shotgun season, Terry had to leave for his construction company's Christmas party just as I was blowing back into camp. Amid all the hectic comings and goings, we stayed in contact. We conducted our planning sessions with our cell phones, and we held firmly to our pact, never wavering. One of us would shoot the mature 9-point, or we'd shoot nothing at all.

Our nephew Jared rolled into camp to film me while Terry was back home partying. That night, another major front blew in, dumping 6 inches of fresh snow on the 12 inches we already had on the ground. I couldn't believe it, but it actually got colder. The mercury plunged into the single digits, the wind howled at 30 to 40 mph, and the wind chill dropped off the charts.

"How in the world have you guys been hunting in these conditions?" Jared asked as we jumped in my truck and headed for the farm.

"It's brutal, man," I laughed, "but you're young and tough, you can handle it." I had no doubt that he could.

We rounded an icy bend in the road, and I spotted some horses feeding in a pasture. I poked Jared and said, "Grandpa Ritter always used to tell me, 'Watch the livestock, they'll tell you what the deer are doing.'" A good omen? We would soon find out.

We sneaked in and climbed into the box blind, which was becoming sort of a home away from home for me, though a frigid and drafty one. Actually, it felt as though we were sitting in a refrigerator. Every time we took a breath, the steam froze on our lips and noses. At least we didn't have to wait too long for the action to heat up.

At about 3:45 p.m., we spotted deer moving back in the timber, their dark coats popping off the snow cover like neon lights. Several does hopped a wire fence, ran 50 yards into the field and chowed down. I kept glassing the woods. More deer were coming, and one of them had a big rack.

"There's a giant by the fence in the woods, getting ready to step out," I whispered to Jared. With the camera already rolling, he was all over it.

Suddenly, a huge gust of wind blew across the field, kicking up beanstalks and turning the already nervous does inside out. They jumped straight up into the air and ran back for the timber, practically running over the buck.

"Oh my God, I can't believe it," I said to Jared as the tall-racked 9-point melted back into the woods.

Once again, we had him right there in our icy grasp, and once again he slipped through our frozen fingers.

We sat another hour, shivering to the bone, flinching every time another arctic gust rattled our blind. I really didn't know how much more I could stand. The breaking point was drawing near. I checked my watch; it was 5 p.m. In an hour we'd be out of here, thawing out yet again.

I looked back toward the fence and screeched, "Big deer, ooh that's him!"

This evening, the power of food had been too much. The big 9-point strode back into

beans and ate like a hog. His body looked huge and black, and his rack soared high against the backdrop of glimmering snow.

It was a long shot for a slug gun, about 150 yards, but I was confident. Once you make the firm decision to shoot a buck, you should not fool around and start second guessing yourself.

I fired. The buck's hind legs kicked high into the air, and that's always a good sign. He bolted back into the timber.

I slumped back in my chair, still frozen on the outside but now

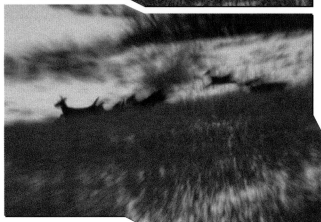

warming nicely on the inside. Mentally, I was just about shot.

We drove back to camp, thawed and watched Jared's video. It was fantastic work for a normal day and spectacular stuff considering the extreme conditions.

"Mark, you hit him perfect, square through the shoulders," Jared roared, "Let's go get him."

First I had to call Terry. He picked up the phone, and above the din of music and people partying, he shouted, "Did you get him, or are you just frozen?"

"You won't believe it," I said. "The big 9-point was just walking out into the beans when the field cleared again. Then he came back. Ten days we've hunted that buck, Terry, 10 days! And we got him!"

"Way to go, guys, give Jared my best for a super job, I can't wait to see the footage," Terry said before hanging up and getting back to his guests.

The tone in my brother's voice said it all. He was as happy for me as if he had just shot the mega buck himself. It doesn't matter who drops the bowstring, pulls the trigger or runs the camera. When Terry or I or any of our friends kills a big deer on video for Drury

Outdoors, it's totally a team effort.

Jared and I bundled up, headed out to the farm and trudged through the knee-deep snow to the timber's edge where the buck fled. We followed the bright-red blood deep into the 260-acre block until we came to a huge crater. We looked straight down, and there he was, a beautiful, thick-bodied, 156-inch buck! I let out a yell that echoed though the chilled timber, then slid down into the hole after him. Finally, after a year, I got to put my hands on the gorgeous creature.

Then the work began. Slipping and sliding in the snow, we wrestled the buck up and out of the hole. The drag out was worse. It took hours, and we slid up and over snow-covered logs and around trees and brush. A little snow is great for sliding a deer, but when it's too deep, the job becomes incredibly tough. The big buck kept sinking, and we had to pull his 220 pounds against the resisting snow.

We were at the breaking point at 10 p.m. The wind had calmed, stars twinkled overhead and the mercury had dropped like a rock. It was below zero, we were tired and famished, and we just couldn't take it anymore. We left the deer, drove back to camp, and collapsed on our warm beds.

The next morning, the temperature hovered around zero, but at least the northwest wind was light and the sun was coming up pink and bright. We pulled and lugged the frozen buck out of the snowy woods and across the ice-crusted bean field. Finally, the truck was in sight. With one final thrust, we hog-wrestled the old 9-point into the truck bed.

I looked at Jared and smiled, and we high-fived. I cannot remember a time when I was so cold, physically exhausted and mentally drained. But I was also so happy.

LESSONS LEARNED

Food-Source Preference. Terry and I pay close and special attention to what deer nibble on at different times of the year, and that has played a key role in our food-plot strategies. If we plan to hunt a farm a lot during the rut, we plant large amounts of green food sources that deer prefer in October and November. If, however, we know we're not going to visit a property until December, we plant vastly different types of seeds. We hunt our main farms throughout October, November and December and many food sources. As Terry has mentioned several times in this book, I've become sort of a mad scientist when it comes to food plots. I'm constantly experimenting, trying to mix and match greens and crops to the times of year that deer eat them most heavily. It's fun, and I enjoy it immensely.

We plant a lot of green food sources, like Biologic Maximum and Clover Plus, on farms that we bowhunt early in the season and into the rut. Interspersed in and around those plots, we often plant winter wheat and Buck Forage oats. We "strip" plant. We might sow a strip of wheat 14 feet wide, butt it up against the edge of a Biologic plot and then plant another strip of oats. Deer

Darrell Daigre and Terry with a pair of 150-inch 8-pointers amidst a lush field of Biologic's Maximum. Year round nutritious food is a must to grow big bucks.

RIGHT:
Mark and his wife Tracy pose with a December 26th Christmas buck for Tracy taken in a standing bean field that was interspersed with Biologic's Fall Attractant.

are browsers, and in some ways they feed a lot like you and I. You go to a salad bar and try a lot of different things — lettuce, carrots, whatever. We try to give deer the same type of smorgasbord.

Another thing we've learned is that green is where it's at early in the season. Here in the Midwest, deer will walk through a standing bean field in October or November to get to a green food source like Biologic. In December, they will often run past the green feed to get to the beans and corn if the weather is cold and snowy.

Although I have become totally consumed with food plots, I never forget to monitor the mast crop, especially acorns, on all of our farms. Acorns are the No. 1 food choice of whitetails anywhere; the nuts are a great, tasty source of protein for deer. If you're not seeing many deer on your plots in October, it's probably because a nearby oak is dropping a heavy crop of acorns.

Our plantings for late-season hunting are based around three different food sources. The two most important are corn and soybeans, with beans probably being No. 1. Deer prefer the beans to anything else in

December, particularly when it's snowy and seasonably cold.

Not every December is created equal. From region to region and from year to year, you don't always have those cold temperatures and heavy snowfalls. When that's the case, deer hardly hit the beans at all. That's why we also plant some green food sources, like Biologic Cover Plus or Maximum, winter wheat or Buck Forage oats.

When the first ponds, creeks and puddles freeze over in early December, there's little natural green forage around, even though there might not be any snow cover. Green plants attract deer and provide them with a good source of moisture. Over the past few years, we have discovered the water content of green plants can be a huge drawing card for whitetails in December.

In short, we plant beans and corn predominantly — probably 80

Old Man Winter can freeze many of the whitetail's water sources in early December. It is during this period that green food plots can pay huge dividends.

We constantly monitor food sources to keep track of the hottest fields throughout the seasons.

percent — on the farms we hunt late in the season. However, we don't turn a blind eye toward green food sources, which comprise about 20 percent of our plantings.

A major point I need to make is we see more mature bucks — and by mature I mean $4\frac{1}{2}$ years old and older — in December and January than we do in October and November. During the rut, big deer burn up a lot of fuel and eventually run out of gas. In December, staring down the barrel of a long, tough winter, they go back to the filling station and hammer high-energy foods like beans

and corn. We take advantage of that weakness. Whitetails truly are slaves to their stomachs, and it's never more obvious than in December.

What's more, if you put out enough seed and plant it right, you will not only see most of the deer that live on your farm, you will also draw bucks from all around. Late in the season, when all the natural forage is gone and gun pressure hits adjoining lands, your land suddenly becomes a safe haven for mature bucks. The big deer come there for one reason: food.

LEFT: Corn is high in carbohydrates and offers extreme palatability especially after a field has been cut.

BELOW: Milo is another high-carbohydrate food source. It has a high drought tolerance and will yield in less than perfect soil conditions.

INSET:
We film throughout October and November with high anticipation of rutting bucks. In December our focus switches to food source.

BELOW:
We see more deer in December than any other time. Any standing bean field is a magnet.

The colder and snowier it is in December, the more whopper bucks you'll see. Terry and I will take 2 inches of snow, but we prefer 5 or 6 inches, which thoroughly covers all the leftover acorns and other woodland foodstuffs. That causes deer to pour into our fields. Deer movement is usually magical ahead of, during and after a fresh snowfall.

Here in the Midwest, Terry and I prefer daytime highs not to exceed 20 or 25 degrees. When you have 40- or 50-degree temperatures, late-season hunting is not nearly as good. The more threatening the conditions, with snow and highs in the teens and 20s, the

better your chances, because more deer get on their feet and move toward food sources. On that brutal mid-December hunt when I killed the big 9-point, we had 40 to 60 deer, including some other nice bucks, coming to the fields every night.

I don't want to leave the impression that every time it gets cold and snows, old, big-racked bucks will show up on a food plot at the drop of a hat. Actually, my hunt for the 9-point reveals just the opposite.

When that buck was 3 1/2 years old, I saw him every night. He came to the bean field as if he was on a regular dinner schedule, regardless of the weather conditions. But when the buck turned 4 1/2, we only saw him twice at the beans, and it took snow and brutally cold temperatures to put him there during legal shooting hours. Physiologically, bucks can really change between 3 1/2 and 4 1/2. Some bucks go underground by the time they reach 4 1/2 years.

Finally, I ought to mention that whitetails prefer cut fields as opposed to standing crops. When you or a farmer harvests a field, all the residue, be it beans or corn, sits on the ground, absorbs a little moisture, softens up and becomes palatable to deer. Also, it's

LEFT: Cut bean fields seem to be highly attractive especially in late November and early December. Any food pressure in open fields is highly dependent upon weather conditions.

BELOW: The doe harvest is the most critical part of any sound management plan. Too many mouths at the table reduce available nutrition in the critical months of January, February, and March.

ABOVE: There is no substitute for the whitetail's number one food source, acorns! Our food plot sightings are directly related to any given year's acorn crop.

RIGHT: Tracks in a field don't lie. We rely more on fresh tracks than any other type of sign. We pay special attention to their size. Big tracks are key clues to a buck's whereabouts.

much easier for does and bucks to move and feed in a low-cut field of corn or beans.

Planting Tactics. Go get a soil test before you plant anything. If the pH of your soil isn't right, plants won't have the proper nutrients, and they won't be supremely palatable to deer. We spend our money on lime and fertilizer to get our ground perfect. You should too. If you don't, you'll waste a lot of cash planting marginal food plots.

I'm really funky about how I plant grain. I guess it's just the mad scientist coming out in me again! I use corn and even soybeans to funnel deer. Here's how it works.

Whether I'm planting a huge field or a 5-acre plot, I typically plant corn or beans 25 to 30 yards off a timber edge where I have a bow stand, or near a particular tree where I plan on hanging a stand in fall. Next, I plant a thin strip of green in the 25 to 30 yards of open ground between the grain and the stand. That might be a combination of clover and Biologic Maximum, or Buck Forage oats and Maximum. Deer often browse along the fringe of grain and eventually work toward the low, green stuff. The edge of the grain, especially if it's standing corn, and the edge of timber create a natural funnel right to your stand.

Amy Reisner with her first buck, a magnificent 4-year-old that weighed 245 pounds in December. Amy passed shots at three other 130- to 150-inch bucks before being rewarded with this mature wall-hanger. Management works!

It's a five-part process. First, look at the predominant wind direction. Second, hang your tree stand. Third, plant the grain. Fourth, plant the green strip. And fifth, fertilize heavily right next to your stand. Try it. It can lead to a shot at a huge buck when the wind is right.

We also plant corn and beans with late-season gun-hunting in mind. We typically sow grain and create edges, corners and openings 40 to 150 yards from our best shotgun and muzzleloader stands.

We also frost-seed clover or Biologic Clover Plus in February and March. We do it based on previous deer observations. If we notice deer walk through a CRP field or a grassy area that's too steep or rough to plow into a food plot, we'll go in and frost-seed, sprinkling seeds close to spots where we have bow stands. The clover will take, and you'll have a wonderfully nutritious and palatable food source for does and bucks next fall. Mow the clover in September. Come October, fresh, lush growth will appear, and whitetails will find it.

We like to plant food plots and frost-seed clover as close as possible to thick bedding areas where we know huge bucks hang out. By nestling high-quality feed tight to a sacred ground, we believe it gives us a fighting chance of seeing a big deer on his feet during daylight. One thing we never do is bust a doe in a plot like that. If you expect to see a lot of buck movement

Our nephew Jared Lurk with a 4$\frac{1}{2}$-year-old 160-inch 11-pointer. This buck was taken in December amidst a field of Biologic's Clover Plus.

in and around your plots, you can't do a lot of shooting there, especially with a gun.

However, to implement a sound deer-management program on your land, you have to kill a lot of does. Too many mouths at the dinner table reduce the available nutrition during the critical months of January, February and March.

So plant a food plot or two just for the purpose of harvesting does. Terry and I do it on all our farms. Plant your "doe plots" as far away as possible from your best big-buck spots. You must shoot does; just do it in the right places.

We always plant our food plots, especially the ones we hunt for mature bucks, where they are practically invisible from a county road. We don't want the noise and pressure of cars going by, and we sure don't want to create a temptation for a poacher or would-be poacher. If you can hide your food plots, do it. Or plant corn and leave the stalks standing close to a road to block the view.

Maybe you don't have the farm implements or the time to plant food plots. Well, if you've got permission to hunt a farm, do the next best thing. Ask the farmer, "Do you mind if I buy two or three acres of your standing crop so I've got a food source to base my hunting around this fall?" Most farmers will sell you that food. If a landowner agrees, inquire further: "By the way, would you mind harvesting about 20 or 30 yards of the crop right next to my bow stand on the edge of the timber

LEFT: Observation in December and January is paramount to success. We are extremely conservative about when we'll actually go hunt a spot. Pressure in the late season is very detrimental.

BELOW: Another ascension to 20 feet. Gun hunting late season food plots is one of our most productive means of harvesting mature bucks.

and leave the rest standing?" That way you'll have a funnel that deer can use to feed right to your stand. Create your own honey hole by buying standing crops from a farmer every now and then. Terry and I have done it quite often over the years.

Deer Management. Terry and I used to look at a buck's rack and say, "He's a shooter, or he's not a shooter." Today, we don't even look at a rack (well, we might peek!). Instead, we study a buck's body and try to determine how old he is. We now manage our deer herds with the goal of shooting only fully mature bucks that are $4\frac{1}{2}$-years-old. We might shoot a $3\frac{1}{2}$-year-old deer with a bow, but not with a gun.

We realize that by doing this, we are creating animals that are extremely difficult to hunt. Bucks are fairly visible when they're $1\frac{1}{2}$ to $3\frac{1}{2}$ years old. Once they hit $4\frac{1}{2}$, the number of hours they move during daylight decreases dramatically. The rut will put the big boys on their feet, and as we've pointed out many times in this chapter, cold, harsh conditions late in the season will find them moving by necessity to food sources. Still, for the most part, fully mature deer are secretive and nocturnal. That's the hard lesson

ABOVE: Severely cold temperatures help put deer on their feet and onto a food source. We like it when highs are in the teens or twenties, single digits are a bonus.

RIGHT: Nothing stimulates late-season deer more than a freshly fallen December snow. We wait all year for that first major snow event. Movement ahead of, during and behind is usually magical.

they have taught us over the years.

We have evolved as deer hunter/managers, and we feel good about passing bucks and letting them live to full maturity. You can bet that years ago I would have busted that $3^1/_2$-year-old, 135-inch buck the first December night I saw him. But I'm glad I passed him, and as it generally turns out, I had a lot to show for it. The buck grew into a stunning 160-inch slammer with incredible body girth and rack mass. Interestingly, he had a totally different look than when he walked under my stand as a $3^1/_2$-year-old.

When you shoot a $1^1/_2$- or a $2^1/_2$-year-old, you're shooting a buck that has only reached about 50 percent of the potential he will show when he's $4^1/_2$.

It's a sin if your goal is to grow big deer.

Now, if you just seek the thrill of killing deer, knock yourself out. But if you want big-bodied, tall-racked giants on your property, don't shoot the young ones. It's as simple as that.

It might seem that the key to proper herd management is to let bucks grow to age $4^1/_2$ or older. In our opinion, the mistake we see made most often is keying in on bucks and not does. Far and away the majority of our tags each fall get wrapped around the leg of a female deer.

LEFT: Pine and cedar trees are fantastic thermal cover throughout the fall and winter

BELOW: What a joyous sunrise the −4 degree morning after we took this 160-inch buck.

Deer are born at a 1-to-1 ratio. For every 50 button bucks there are 50 doe fawns. We try to keep the numbers on our properties as close to their natural rate as possible. Granted, we are happy with a ratio of two or three adult does for every antlered buck, but we strive for 1:1. Based on the observations alone, you can roughly determine what you're ratio is. We also use trail-monitoring cameras to help us determine the mix.

By constantly striving for a 1:1 ratio, we reduce the number of mouths at the table and enhance the health of our deer herd. Such management also improves the rut's intensity. We certainly are not biologists, but we definitely experience incredible results on our own farms based on a grass-roots, common-sense approach. ■

POSTSCRIPT

In March 2000, nine months before I killed the buck, Jared found one of his sheds. A neighboring farmer had offered to help us plow under the bean field, and he had disked right over the antler. Remarkably, it was still in perfect shape when Jared picked it up. It was undeniably the shed of the 8-point I had passed the previous December. The configuration of the main beam and tines were identical to the left side of the buck I shot, though he had grown a short G-4 on the right side and had picked up a lot of overall mass and tine length.

Most interestingly, Jared had found the shed within 50 yards of where I shot the buck and where I had passed him the previous December. That proves once again that if you have a plentiful diversity of high-quality food sources on your property, along with thick bedding cover that you stay out of most of the time, a mature buck won't wander very far. To the contrary, he will live right there, and his core area can be extremely small. And you know the coolest part? Every year a buck survives past full maturity, his core area shrinks even more.

∿

CHAPTER TEN

SMILE, YOU'RE ON CANDID CAMERA

Our first encounter with the giant occurred early in the November rut, in the leaden predawn of a chilly day. Nephew Jared and I were slowly driving on a dirt farm road when we caught the shine of eyeballs in the headlights. It was a deer for sure, but no big deal – until Jared barked from beneath his binoculars, "Stop … buck … oh, Mark, he's a monster!"

I rolled the truck to a stop, glassed the deer and let out my little trademark, "Ooohh." I had definitely never seen this brute before. The sight of the chunky beast with the swollen, sagging neck was almost surreal in the eerie fluorescent glow.

▓ Trail-monitoring cameras are one of the hottest innovations to hit store shelves in years. One fall, a giant $6\frac{1}{2}$- or $7\frac{1}{2}$-year-old buck graced our TrailMAC lenses three times and our video cameras four times. His fourth appearance on video proved to be his last. We'll relive the tale of the awesome, photogenic buck, then Terry and I will share our secrets for taking quality trail-camera photos and using cameras to get the drop on big deer.

Drunk on testosterone and tending a hot doe, he stood in one spot, drooling and slowly nodding his blocky head. He paid us absolutely no mind, and I took advantage. I eased out of the truck, hand-held my video camera and shot two minutes of footage before the doe broke and the loopy monster lumbered off in hot pursuit.

About a week later, Jared and I watched incredulously as the buck moved onto a food plot at dusk. The buck, obviously a stud if not "the stud" of these parts, was dogging another hot doe. The doe darted to within 300 yards – then 200, then 100 – dragging the buck toward our stand. I hadn't gotten a good look at the buck's rack during our predawn encounter, but now I gasped at the sight of a massive 160-class 11-pointer. His rack had spectacular points and a forked G-2 on the right side. My mind raced, my stomach churned,

and my heart nearly pounded out of my chest as I put tension on the bowstring. "I've only seen this giant twice in my life and now we're going to kill him," I whispered to myself as the doe stepped within 50 yards of our stand.

Then, for some inexplicable reason, the doe veered right and into the timber, snatching the buck out of our grasp. The buck disappeared just like that, and I had serious doubts we would ever see him again. I slumped back in my stand and sat in silence as the still, chilly darkness enveloped up. I cannot remember ever being so depressed. It isn't often that you get an opportunity at a mature deer with a bow, much less a totally mature animal. It's a crusher when a monster is right there one second and gone the next.

The next morning, our friend Darrell Daigre, vice president of Mossy Oak, sat in a stand on the edge of a soybean field, about 200 yards from where the buck had walked into the timber the previous night. Darrell had shot a good buck the previous afternoon. Rather than sleeping, he graciously helped us by scouting with his binoculars and video camera. As we have stated many times in this book, the more time you and your friends are afield observing deer, the

better off you'll be, providing the wind is right. Well, this just proves our point once again. Incredibly, the hot doe dragged the giant 11-point past Darrell at 10 steps. He kept his wits and shot some outstanding footage.

We had a large crew in camp. After the morning hunt, we went straight to the "video war room." It's one of the coolest things about our business. After each morning and evening hunt, whether we shoot a deer or not, we gather and watch/critique each other's footage. Most of the footage is steady and tack-sharp — except sometimes for Terry's! Anyway, two tapes – Darrell's and Jared's from the previous evening – were the highlights of this screening.

I vividly recall everyone hovering over the monitor to watch the awesome footage. We couldn't get enough of the 11-point, and we rewound the tapes repeatedly. The buck's 160-inch rack was one thing, but my word, his body and maturity! They were striking, almost to the point of being appalling. The deer had incredible girth around the shoulders, along with a telltale sagging belly. His neck was rut-swollen to the point of looking absurd. Loose skin hung off his neck and blocky face. His sides and hindquarters showed rubbed patches and other battle scars, although none of us could imagine what kind of buck would pick a fight with this beast – maybe an 8- or 10-point stud in his prime, thinking this old warrior was going downhill.

"Mark, that's quite possibly the oldest buck we've ever filmed," Terry bellowed, his eyes sparkling with excitement. "I bet he's 6 $\frac{1}{2}$, or older."

"Yeah, and where in the world did he come from?" I shouted.

"We've hunted up here for years, and nobody has ever seen that hog. Now we've filmed him three times in a week. It's amazing!"

As the tapes of the giant 11 kept rolling, our crew batted around several theories concerning the brute's sudden appearance. The buck might have been living right under our noses for years, almost totally nocturnal. He might have slipped in from a neighboring farm to court does. Or, the old devil might have suddenly and permanently moved his home core area from an adjoining property to ours, having tired of the competition from other mature bucks or the intense hunting pressure. Terry and I believe fully mature bucks do that a lot more than people realize. That is, they return to an area where they might have lived for two or three years before broadening their range. Then, as they age or sense the need to survive, they return home. Whatever the case, it made for a lively deer-camp discussion. The big boy was here, and we badly wanted to harvest him.

Over the next three weeks, Terry and I, along with several friends and guests, spent a lot of time hunting and scouting the farm. We saw a lot of good bucks and shot a couple of dandies. But nobody laid eyes on the ancient 11-point. Had he returned home to a neighboring farm once the rut was over? Had he turned as nocturnal as a vampire once again? Years ago, we would have been left to ponder and speculate on such things, but no more. We still had our eye on the giant, just in a totally different and secretive way.

Over the past few years, Terry and I have really gotten into trail-monitoring cameras. They are a blast to use; they're incredibly effective scouting tools. That's why we've gone whole hog with our trail-camera strategy. We've scattered cameras all over our farms, and we capture more than 4,500 photos each fall.

When chasing the giant 11-point, we snapped flash photos of him three times: Nov. 21, 24 and Dec. 1. The nocturnal critter popped up on three different cameras in three different places. Appalled by the bucks' gaudy maturity, we studied the photos and

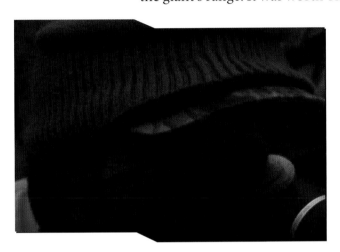

narrowed his core area down to roughly 1¹/₂ square miles (960 acres). He was still on our farm and living right there! The stand where Darrell last videotaped the buck lay smack in the middle of the giant's range. It was worth one last shot in mid-December. This time I would be hunting my trusty Remington Model 700 muzzleloader. That extended my range out to 150 yards. So, if he showed, we'd have a chance.

Terry and I climbed to the stand and questioned our sanity. It was one of those miserable, bone-chilling, wind-blown afternoons. The western sky was the color of a deep bruise; any minute it could open up and pour – certainly not something you want when you've got a camera and a black-powder rifle in your hands. Besides, we were very skeptical. Bucks might not move during low pressure, but then again the nasty weather might put them on their feet looking for food. When in doubt, throw on your rain gear and go for it, especially when the season is winding down or your days afield are limited. You never know what might happen.

"Boy, it sure would be nice to see that old 11-point," I whispered to Terry as we settled in, peeking up at the dark sky, hoping it would not open up and drown us.

He nodded as he checked his camera's settings, but the look on his face said, "Fat chance."

Then, 15 minutes later…

"I see tines," I whispered, shiver-

ing and raising my binoculars. "That's a giant, Terry. A giant buck!"

The deer appeared from a wooded draw, following a group of nine does. "It's him!" Terry hissed. You couldn't miss that gaudy old body and the forked G2 on his right antler.

As I locked in on one of the oldest buck's I had ever seen, I could only imagine what my brother was going through. I had been there and done that many times, and it's never easy. You have to control your emotions, stay focused, hold the camera steady, don't flinch when the shooter pulls the trigger, pan and stay on the buck as he kicks and crashes away. It's tough on a good day, and darn difficult during horrendous filming conditions.

Terry could handle it, but could I? I shook like a leaf. The chilling mist and the sight of the enormous buck took me to near hyperventilation. I breathed deeply a few times and whispered "Calm down!" The buck was about 90 yards away, skulking to my left. I locked the cross-hairs on his gray shoulder and pressed the trigger. A huge plume of gray smoke roiled into the air and blended into the gray-black sky.

"Down! He just went down – I heard him crash!" I growled with intensity I seldom show. You never know what will pop out of your mouth when you shoot a huge buck.

The shot was perfect, through both lungs, and the deer ran less than 100 yards. Darkness was approaching, and the dark sky's ceil-

ing was lowering fast, creating an ominous gloom. Racing the clock, Terry and I wrestled the gargantuan buck up out of the draw, across the beans and into my pickup truck. Seconds after we pulled into the tractor barn, the skies opened up and rain pounded the metal roof.

We chattered like kids while admiring the buck. We were more stunned and appalled than ever at the sight of his barrel chest, low belly, thick, sagging hide, squin-ty eyes and gnarly rack. "He's at least 6 $^1/_2$ and maybe 7 or 8, who knows?" Terry yelled over the din of the downpour.

I just nodded. What more was there to say? Any buck that lives that long these days is the trophy of a lifetime, regardless of what his rack scores. And this bruiser would score into the 160s.

The rain didn't let up, and we decided to wait for morning and better weather to shoot the closing segment of our video. But that was fine by us. It would make the final filming of the old warrior that much sweeter.

LESSONS
LEARNED

The Power of Observation. In Chapter 2, we detailed our varied and often extreme tactics for observing deer. We won't repeat that here, but we will once again shout our manta: Observe more and hunt less for more success! The hunt for the giant 11-point just reinforces that point once more.

I videotaped that monster once in the November predawn. The next week, Jared and Darrell got their incredible, close-range footage. Those video segments, along with the three trail-camera photos gave us six solid sightings of the buck in a 1½-mile area over the course of a month. That was important, because those images caused us to hang tough and keep hunting one of the most impressive bucks we had ever seen. Even better, those six observations told us where the buck was living, and they helped us pinpoint his core area. It ultimately led us straight to the stand where we filmed the deer for the seventh and final time.

We just can't make the point too many times. The more you study whitetails, the better your chances of hanging stands in just the right spots to see and kill mature bucks. It is without a doubt one of the most

Our TrailMAC cameras have provided so many wonderful images of bucks that we had no idea existed in our area.

important lessons Terry and I have learned in our obsessive quest for mature deer.

Trail-Camera Tactics. We began using trail-monitoring cameras a few years ago, and they have changed our lives. The cameras are a blast to use. You shiver with excitement every time you remove an exposed roll of film from a box on a tree. You pace the floor as the one-hour photo guy or gal processes the film. You tear into the package and smile at the shots of does, young bucks, bobcats, turkeys, etc. You crack a wide grin and let out a yell when you get a snapshot of a mature deer, especially a nocturnal bruiser you've never seen before.

We use TrailMAC flash cameras by Trail Sense Engineering that enable us to photograph deer up to 60 feet away. We go with 400-speed, 36-exposure film. We don't recommend 24-exposure film because you have to keep sneaking back into a spot to change film too often. One of the best things about a trail camera is it allows you to scout and monitor an area

RIGHT: We try to only change film during the midday so as not to put unwanted pressure on our hunting areas.

BELOW: Open fence gaps are great locations to place cameras for good, close shots of deer. We try to place cameras where approaching deer will pass within 10 to 30 feet of the unit.